ARRIVAL
01-JUL-2008

D0955336

HOW TO BE AN AMERICAN

A FIELD GUIDE TO
CITIZENSHIP

SILVIA HIDALGO

ABRAMS IMAGE, NEW YORK

TABLE OF CONTENTS

INTRODUCTION

On March 20th, 2018, I went to vote; it was my first time voting as a U.S. citizen. Voting has always been important to me. I was born in Costa Rica, where elections are celebrated with the same enthusiasm and sometimes fanaticism that only very important soccer matches receive.

In 2015, I decided to start the American naturalization process. I had been here for sixteen years, and every election day, when I watched others head to the polls, I said to myself, "too many years without voting have gone by." I picked up the material for the test and I immediately knew I was going to have to go back to my old studying tricks in order to prepare for the exam.

As a teenager, I made elaborate summaries to study for tests. These were pages filled with information mixed with doodles, arrows pointing at jokes, infographics with expressive type—all useful pieces to help my brain visually learn and remember the information. Soon after I started working on my citizenship summary, I realized it was something I could share with other people preparing for the same process.

Through the wonderful magic of people connecting with people, I got the chance to share my forty-page booklet with Abrams. The day I became a citizen, I came back home and received a phone call giving me the wonderful news that my booklet was going to be a real book! It could be bigger and it could be for everyone!

So, who is this book for? This book is for you, future citizen. It will help you prepare for the naturalization test, but most importantly, it will tell you about this country, about its beginnings, its history; it will also give you information to help you understand the American political system and how to be an active and involved citizen.

This book is also for you, old citizen. It's an entertaining refresher course on many things you learned when you were a kid and probably forgot. It talks about this country's ideals and the people who have fought to defend them; it talks about the importance of protecting and celebrating our democracy and the power American citizens have had in shaping the history of the United States.

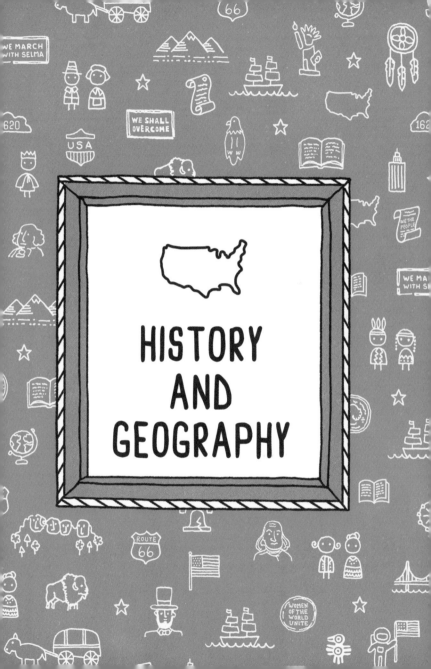

HISTORY
AND
GEOGRAPHY

LIVED IN THE TERRITORY NOW KNOWN AS THE UNITED STATES

BEFORE THEY CAME

SOME AMERICAN INDIANS HAD PERFECTED THE RAISING OF CORN AND OTHER VEGETABLES AND FRUITS, AS WELL AS PEANUTS, CHOCOLATE, AND TOBACCO.

IN SOME TRIBES THEY WERE USING IRRIGATION CANALS AND DAMS, MAKING CERAMICS, WEAVING BASKETS, AND USING COTTON TO MAKE CLOTHING.

COLONISTS FROM ENGLAND

IN THE EARLY 1600s COLONISTS CAME TO AMERICA

THEY SAILED ACROSS THE ATLANTIC OCEAN FLEEING PERSECUTION
AND LOOKING TO CREATE A BETTER COUNTRY FOR THEMSELVES.
THE PEOPLE OF PLYMOUTH COUNTY WERE LOOKING FOR:

ECONOMIC
OPPORTUNITY

RELIGIOUS
FREEDOM

POLITICAL
FREEDOM

13 ORIGINAL COLONIES

PENNSYLVANIA
NORTH CAROLINA
SOUTH CAROLINA
NEW HAMPSHIRE
MASSACHUSETTS BAY
RHODE ISLAND

MARYLAND
VIRGINIA
GEORGIA
NEW YORK
CONNECTICUT
NEW JERSEY
DELAWARE

COLONIAL ELITE

A GROUP OF VERY FEW PEOPLE OWNED LAND AND SERVANTS, HELD INFLUENTIAL POLITICAL POSITIONS, AND HAD A GOOD RELATIONSHIP WITH THE CHURCH.

INDENTURED SERVANTS

MORE THAN HALF THE EUROPEAN COLONISTS CAME AS SERVANTS, RUNNING AWAY FROM EXTREME POVERTY. THEY AGREED TO WORK SEVEN YEARS OF HARD LABOR IN EXCHANGE FOR LAND AND FREEDOM.

AMERICAN INDIAN TRIBES

APACHE
ARAWAK
BLACKFEET
CHEROKEE
CHEYENNE

CHIPPEWA
CHOCTAW
CREEK
CROW
HOPI

INUIT
IROQUOIS
MOHEGAN
NAVAJO
ONEIDA

PUEBLO
SEMINOLE
SHAWNEE
SIOUX

CULTURE AREAS

 NORTHWEST COAST

 GREAT BASIN

 CALIFORNIA

 PLAINS

 SOUTHWEST

 NORTHEAST

 PLATEAU

 SOUTHEAST

AMERICAN INDIANS

DESPITE HAVING SUPERIOR FIREARMS, COLONISTS COULDN'T ENSLAVE THE AMERICAN INDIANS. THE NATIVE POPULATION WAS BIGGER, MORE RESOURCEFUL, DEFIANT, AND KNEW THE TERRITORY WELL.

PEOPLE FROM AFRICA

ENSLAVED

DURING THE 17TH AND 18TH CENTURIES MEN, WOMEN, AND CHILDREN
WERE BROUGHT FROM AFRICA TO AMERICA AGAINST THEIR WILL.
THEIR CULTURE, LANGUAGE, FAMILY, AND COMMUNITY RELATIONS WERE
WIPED OUT AND REPLACED WITH A LIFE OF EXTREMELY HARD FORCED
LABOR AND INHUMANE CONDITIONS IN A FOREIGN LAND.

SLAVERY IN AMERICA

THE FIRST AFRICAN SLAVES WERE BROUGHT TO JAMESTOWN, VIRGINIA, IN 1619 TO FARM LUCRATIVE CROPS LIKE TOBACCO, RICE, AND INDIGO.

IN 1641 SLAVERY WAS LEGALIZED. AFRICAN PEOPLE BECAME PERSONAL PROPERTY AND VALUABLE COMMODITIES. THEY HAD NO LEGAL RIGHTS, AND ABUSE AND VIOLENCE TOWARD THEM WAS ENCOURAGED.

SLAVES WERE BROUGHT FROM FOUR MAIN REGIONS IN AFRICA:

MEN AND WOMEN WERE SOLD AS PART OF THE WORK FORCE. LIGHT-SKINNED YOUNG WOMEN, OFTEN CALLED FANCY GIRLS, WERE SOLD AS MISTRESSES OR FOR PROSTITUTION.

 SENEGAMBIA:
NOW SENEGAL, GAMBIA, GUINEA-BISSAU, AND MALI

 GOLD COAST:
NOW GHANA AND IVORY COAST

 BIGHT OF BIAFRA:
NOW EASTERN NIGERIA AND CAMEROON

 WEST-CENTRAL AFRICA:
NOW ANGOLA, REPUBLIC OF CONGO, DEMOCRATIC REPUBLIC OF THE CONGO, AND GABON

THE AMERICAN REVOLUTION

THE BRITISH TAXED THE COLONISTS WITHOUT THEIR CONSENT AND THE
COLONISTS HAD NOBODY TO RESPRESENT THEM IN THE BRITISH GOVERMENT.
THE ENGLISH EMPIRE WAS FORCING COLONISTS TO LET BRITISH SOLDIERS
SLEEP AND EAT IN THEIR HOMES.

THE DECLARATION OF INDEPENDENCE

IT ANNOUNCED THE UNITED STATES'S INDEPENDENCE FROM BRITAIN. IT WAS ADOPTED ON

JULY 4, **1776**.

IT DECLARED THAT ALL MEN ARE CREATED EQUAL AND HAVE THE RIGHT TO · · · · · · · · · · · · · ·

IN CONGRESS, JULY 4, 1776.

A DECLARATION

BY THE REPRESENTATIVES OF THE

UNITED STATES OF AMERICA,

IN GENERAL CONGRESS ASSEMBLED

LIFE, LIBERTY, AND THE PURSUIT OF HAPPINESS

JOHN HANCOCK, PRESIDENT

WRITTEN BY THOMAS JEFFERSON

FOUNDING FATHER

JOHN ADAMS, ROBERT R. LIVINGSTON, ROGER SHERMAN, AND BENJAMIN FRANKLIN HELPED WITH THE DRAFT.

FIRST POSTMASTER GENERAL OF THE U.S.

STARTED THE FIRST FREE LIBRARIES

OLDEST MEMBER OF THE CONSTITUTIONAL CONVENTION

BENJAMIN FRANKLIN

U.S. DIPLOMAT

WRITER OF *Poor Richard's Almanac*

THE CONSTITUTION

IS THE SUPREME LAW OF THE LAND

IT SETS UP AND DEFINES THE GOVERNMENT AND PROTECTS THE BASIC RIGHTS OF AMERICANS.

JAMES MADISON, JOHN JAY, AND ALEXANDER HAMILTON WROTE A SERIES OF ESSAYS AND ARTICLES TO PERSUADE PEOPLE TO RATIFY THE CONSTITUTION. THE FEDERALIST PAPERS DETAILED HOW THE NEW GOVERNMENT WOULD WORK. THEY SUPPORTED THE PASSAGE OF THE CONSTITUTION.

1787

THE FOUNDING FATHERS WROTE THE CONSTITUTION AT THE CONSTITUTIONAL CONVENTION, PRESIDED OVER BY GEORGE WASHINGTON.

FOUNDING FATHER

George Washington

FATHER OF OUR COUNTRY
FIRST PRESIDENT OF THE U.S.

1789 – 1797

····· ◄ WE THE PEOPLE =
SELF-GOVERNMENT

WE NEED TO PROTECT OUR INDIVIDUAL RIGHTS!

WE NEED A BILL OF RIGHTS!

AGREED

1791

THE BILL OF RIGHTS BECAME PART OF THE CONSTITUTION. IT IS MADE UP OF THE FIRST TEN AMENDMENTS TO THE CONSTITUTION. IT LIMITS THE POWER OF THE FEDERAL GOVERNMENT AND PROTECTS THE RIGHTS OF ALL CITIZENS.

THE ANTI-FEDERALISTS

THE ANTI-FEDERALISTS WERE STATES'-RIGHTS ADVOCATES. THEY WERE AGAINST:

- THE AUTHORITY OF A SINGLE NATIONAL GOVERNMENT
- UPPER-CLASS DOMINANCE
- INADEQUATE SEPARATION OF POWERS
- LOSS OF IMMEDIATE CONTROL OVER LOCAL AFFAIRS

ANTI-FEDERALIST INFLUENCE HELPED LEAD TO THE PASSAGE OF THE UNITED STATES BILL OF RIGHTS.

Bill of Rights

Congress of THE United States,

JAMES MADISON
FATHER OF THE BILL OF RIGHTS

FOUNDING FATHER

THE BILL OF RIGHTS WAS WRITTEN BY JAMES MADISON

AN AMENDMENT

IS A CHANGE OR ADDITION TO THE CONSTITUTION. THERE ARE:

27 AMENDMENTS

IN THE CONSTITUTION.

THE COTTON GIN

WAS INVENTED IN 1793

AMERICAN INVENTOR ELI WHITNEY CREATED A MODERN MECHANICAL COTTON GIN. COTTON BECAME A TREMENDOUSLY PROFITABLE BUSINESS FOR THE SOUTH. MASTERS ACQUIRED MORE SLAVES AND STARTED MOVING FROM THE SOUTH TO THE WEST, LOOKING FOR NEW LAND TO FARM.

THE UNION WAS DIVIDED INTO TWO PARTS: THE NORTHERN STATES SUPPORTING THE ABOLISHMENT OF SLAVERY AND THE SOUTHERN STATES THAT WANTED TO KEEP SLAVERY.

FOR MANY, SLAVERY HAD BECOME MORE THAN A POLITICAL OR COMMERCIAL ISSUE; IT HAD BECOME A MORAL ISSUE.

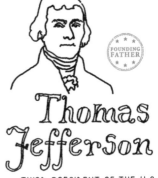

FOUNDING FATHER

Thomas Jefferson

THIRD PRESIDENT OF THE U.S.

1801-1809

ROBERT R. LIVINGSTON AND JAMES MONROE OFFERED FRANCE $10 MILLION FOR THE NEW ORLEANS PORT ON JEFFERSON'S BEHALF. FRANCE SOLD THE U.S. THE LOUISIANA TERRITORY (828 SQUARE MILES) FOR $15 MILLION PLUS INTEREST (TOTAL $27,267,622).

THE
LOUISIANA
PURCHASE

John Adams

SECOND PRESIDENT OF THE U.S.

1797-1801

AND FIRST VICE PRESIDENT

Alexander Hamilton

FIRST SECRETARY OF THE TREASURY
OF THE UNITED STATES OF AMERICA

1789-1795

STRONG PROPONENT OF THE
FEDERALIST FORM OF GOVERNMENT
(STRONG CENTRALIZED GOVERNMENT)

John Jay

FIRST CHIEF OF JUSTICE OF
THE SUPREME COURT

1789-1795

TRAIL OF TEARS

MANY WHITE SETTLERS LIVING ON THE WESTERN FRONTIER WANTED TO RELOCATE TO THE LAND OWNED BY AMERICAN INDIAN TRIBES IN GEORGIA, ALABAMA, NORTH CAROLINA, FLORIDA, AND TENNESSEE. THEY PRESSURED AND HARRASSED THE TRIBES BY STEALING THEIR LIVESTOCK, LOOTING AND BURNING THEIR HOUSES AND TOWNS, AND SQUATTING ON THEIR LAND. SETTLERS WANTED TO GROW COTTON, AND THE LAND WAS BECOMING MORE DESIRED AS MORE SETTLERS WERE COMING TO THE UNITED STATES. IN 1829, GOLD WAS FOUND ON CHEROKEE LAND IN GEORGIA AND SPECULATORS PRESSED THE GOVERNMENT TO GET INVOLVED.

THE INDIAN REMOVAL ACT OF 1830

- IT GAVE THE FEDERAL GOVERNMENT THE POWER TO FORCIBLY EVICT ALL THE INDIAN TRIBES LOCATED EAST OF THE MISSISSIPPI RIVER AND MOVE THEM TO LAND IN THE WEST: THE "INDIAN COLONIZATION ZONE" OR "INDIAN TERRITORY" (PRESENT-DAY OKLAHOMA).
- THE GOVERNMENT AGREED TO PROVIDE AID FOR TRANSPORTATION AND LOGISTICAL SUPPORT DURING AND AFTER THE TRIBES' JOURNEY.
- THE ACT WAS SIGNED BY PRESIDENT ANDREW JACKSON.

BETWEEN 1830 AND 1850, PEOPLE FROM THE CREEK, CHEROKEE, CHOCTAW, CHICKASAW, AND SEMINOLE TRIBES WERE FORCED FROM THEIR LAND. OVER 3,500 CREEK AND 4,000 CHEROKEE DIED DURING THE JOURNEY.

SOME TRIBES AGREED TO THE TERMS OF THE EXCHANGE AND PEACEFULLY HEADED WEST, BUT LACK OF EXPERIENCE AND CORRUPTION IN THE GOVERNMENT CAUSED MANY OF THEM TO DIE OF MALNUTRITION, EXHAUSTION, EXPOSURE, AND DISEASE WHILE TRAVELING.

THE CHEROKEE TOOK THE CASE TO THE SUPREME COURT AND WON, BUT IT DIDN'T MATTER. PRESIDENT JACKSON SENT TROOPS TO ROUND THEM UP AT GUNPOINT AND FORCED THEM OUT OF THEIR LAND.

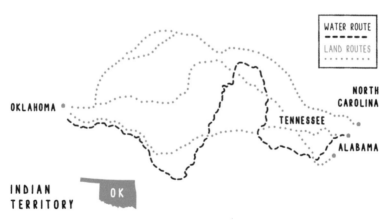

WATER ROUTE
- - - - - -
LAND ROUTES
. . . .

NORTH CAROLINA

OKLAHOMA

TENNESSEE

ALABAMA

INDIAN TERRITORY

OK

THE GOVERNMENT PROMISED THE TRIBES THEIR NEW LAND WOULD REMAIN UNTOUCHED, BUT IN 1907 OKLAHOMA BECAME A STATE AND THE INDIAN TERRITORY WAS DISSOLVED.

THE UNDERGROUND RAILROAD

WAS A COLLECTION OF INDIVIDUALS AND GROUPS WHO HELPED RUNAWAY SLAVES ESCAPE TO FREEDOM. THE NETWORK OF ROUTES EXTENDED THROUGH 23 STATES TO THE PROMISED LAND: CANADA.

THOSE WHO HELPED WERE MEMBERS OF THE FREE BLACK COMMUNITY, NORTHERN ABOLITIONISTS, PHILANTHROPISTS, AND CHURCH LEADERS, MANY OF THEM QUAKERS.

David Ruggles

CREATED THE NEW YORK COMMITTEE OF VIGILANCE, AN ORGANIZATION THAT HELPED PROTECT BLACK PEOPLE FROM BEING KIDNAPPED AND SOLD INTO SLAVERY.

Harriet Tubman

AN AMERICAN ABOLITIONIST AND HUMANITARIAN WHO BECAME A CONDUCTOR FOR THE UNDERGROUND RAILROAD AFTER SHE ESCAPED SLAVERY. SHE RISKED HER LIFE MULTIPLE TIMES TO RESCUE FRIENDS AND FAMILY MEMBERS. SHE WAS AN ARMED SCOUT AND SPY DURING THE CIVIL WAR AND AN ACTIVIST FOR WOMEN'S SUFFRAGE.

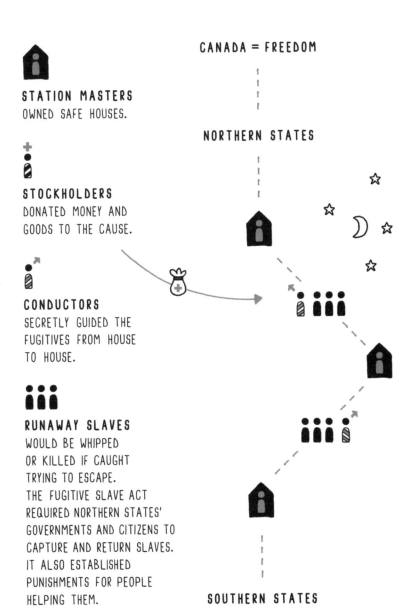

STATION MASTERS
OWNED SAFE HOUSES.

STOCKHOLDERS
DONATED MONEY AND
GOODS TO THE CAUSE.

CONDUCTORS
SECRETLY GUIDED THE
FUGITIVES FROM HOUSE
TO HOUSE.

RUNAWAY SLAVES
WOULD BE WHIPPED
OR KILLED IF CAUGHT
TRYING TO ESCAPE.
THE FUGITIVE SLAVE ACT
REQUIRED NORTHERN STATES'
GOVERNMENTS AND CITIZENS TO
CAPTURE AND RETURN SLAVES.
IT ALSO ESTABLISHED
PUNISHMENTS FOR PEOPLE
HELPING THEM.

CANADA = FREEDOM

NORTHERN STATES

SOUTHERN STATES

THE AMERICAN CIVIL WAR

Abraham Lincoln
1861–1865

ABRAHAM LINCOLN WAS ELECTED PRESIDENT AFTER PROMISING TO ABOLISH SLAVERY.

WANTING TO KEEP THE INSTITUTION OF SLAVERY ALIVE, SEVEN STATES SPLIT OFF FROM THE UNITED STATES TO FORM THEIR OWN COUNTRY CALLED **THE CONFEDERATE STATES OF AMERICA**, WHERE SLAVERY WAS LEGAL.

VIOLENT DISAGREEMENT OVER SLAVERY CAUSED WAR TO BREAK OUT BETWEEN THE NORTHERN STATES (THE UNION) FIGHTING TO END SLAVERY AND THE SOUTHERN STATES (THE CONFEDERACY) SUPPORTING SLAVERY. THE WAR WAS FOUGHT FOR FOUR YEARS.

THERE WERE 620,000 WAR CASUALTIES.

JANUARY 1863
LINCOLN FULFILLED HIS PROMISE BY FREEING ALL SLAVES WITH **THE EMANCIPATION PROCLAMATION.**

JANUARY 1865
CONGRESS PASSED THE 13TH AMENDMENT, ABOLISHING SLAVERY AND INVOLUNTARY SERVITUDE.

APRIL 1865
ABRAHAM LINCOLN WAS ASSASSINATED.

JUNE 1865
THE CIVIL WAR ENDED.

THE WOMEN OF THE CIVIL WAR

SUSAN B. ANTHONY AND ELIZABETH CADY STANTON

WERE SOCIAL REFORMERS, ABOLITIONISTS, AND WOMEN'S RIGHTS ACTIVISTS. DURING THE WAR THEY WORKED ON BEHALF OF THE UNION AND COLLECTED ONE MILLION SIGNATURES ON PETITIONS SUPPORTING THE 13TH AMENDMENT.

ELIZABETH VAN LEW

HAD A NETWORK OF SPIES, MOSTLY WOMEN, SOME OF THEM EVEN WORKING INSIDE THE CONFEDERATE WHITE HOUSE.

FRANCES CLAYTON

DISGUISED HERSELF AS A MAN AND FOUGHT FOR THE UNION NEXT TO HER HUSBAND.

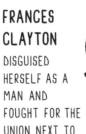

PAULINE CUSHMAN

WAS AN ACTRESS AND A SPY FOR THE UNION. PASSING AS A SYMPATHIZER TO THE CONFEDERACY, SHE WAS ABLE TO GAIN ACCESS TO HIGH-LEVEL CONVERSATIONS AND DOCUMENTS. SHE WAS CAUGHT AND SENTENCED TO DEATH BUT WAS SAVED BY UNION TROOPS.

CIVIL RIGHTS AND ACTIVISM IN AMERICA

THROUGHOUT THE HISTORY OF THE UNITED STATES, ACTIVISTS HAVE SUPPORTED AND DEFENDED THE AMERICAN IDEALS OF FREEDOM AND EQUALITY. THROUGH PROTESTS, PETITIONS, BOYCOTTS, MARCHES, LAWSUITS, FUNDRAISING, AND MANY OTHER ACTIONS, MANY AMERICANS HAVE FOUGHT TO MAKE THIS COUNTRY A BETTER PLACE FOR EVERYONE.

WOMEN'S SUFFRAGE

1848
SENECA FALLS CONVENTION
- ORGANIZED BY ELIZABETH CADY STANTON AND LUCRETIA MOTT. IT WAS THE FIRST WOMEN'S RIGHTS CONVENTION.
- OTHER CONVENTIONS FOLLOWED, PROVIDING A PLATFORM FOR THE BEGINNING OF THE WOMEN'S SUFFRAGE MOVEMENT.

1914
WORLD WAR I
- MANY WOMEN CAMPAIGNED AGAINST THE U.S. JOINING THE WAR.
- OTHERS ENLISTED IN THE ARMED FORCES OR WORKED IN WARTIME INDUSTRIES, FILLING THE JOBS LEFT BY SOLDIERS.

ALICE PAUL
- LEADER OF THE NATIONAL WOMEN'S PARTY.
- JAILED FOR HER ANTI-WAR PROTESTS, AND, WHILE IN JAIL, SHE STARTED A HUNGER STRIKE AND ENDURED FORCED FEEDINGS BY THE AUTHORITIES.

- WOMEN'S PATRIOTISM DURING THE WAR AND PRESSURE COMING FROM MANY ACTIVISTS PUSHED THE PASSAGE OF THE 19TH AMENDMENT.
- IN 1920, AMERICAN WOMEN WERE GRANTED THE RIGHT TO VOTE.

JANE ADDAMS

- PEACE ACTIVIST, SOCIAL WORKER, SOCIOLOGIST, PRESIDENT OF THE WOMEN'S INTERNATIONAL LEAGUE FOR PEACE AND FREEDOM.
- IN 1884, SHE CO-FOUNDED, WITH ELLEN GATES STARR, THE HULL HOUSE IN CHICAGO.

- THIS COMMUNITY PROVIDED SOCIAL AND EDUCATIONAL OPPORTUNITIES FOR WORKING CLASS PEOPLE.
- HULL HOUSE ALSO HELPED WOMEN ACROSS CLASSES BY BRINGING THEM TOGETHER TO WORK IN SOCIAL REFORM.

MARGARET SANGER

- BIRTH CONTROL ACTIVIST, SEX EDUCATOR, WRITER, AND NURSE.
- SHE WAS THE FOUNDER OF THE BIRTH CONTROL MOVEMENT IN THE U.S., OPENED THE FIRST BIRTH CONTROL CLINIC AND FOUNDED THE AMERICAN BIRTH CONTROL LEAGUE, AN ORGANIZATION THAT LATER EVOLVED INTO PLANNED PARENTHOOD.

EMMA GOLDMAN

- ANARCHIST, WRITER, POLITICAL ACTIVIST, AND LECTURER ON WOMEN'S RIGHTS AND SOCIAL ISSUES.
- SHE WAS ARRESTED MANY TIMES FOR SHARING HER VIEWS ON BIRTH CONTROL AND FOR GIVING LESSONS IN PUBLIC ON HOW TO USE CONTRACEPTIVES.
- IN 1919, AFTER SPENDING TWO YEARS IN PRISON, SHE WAS DEPORTED TO RUSSIA.

ROSIE THE RIVETER

- CREATED IN 1943 TO REPRESENT WOMEN WHO WORKED IN FACTORIES AND SHIPYARDS DURING WWII.
- IS USED TODAY AS A SYMBOL OF AMERICAN FEMINISM AND WOMEN'S ECONOMIC POWER.

CIVIL RIGHTS MOVEMENT

A MASS PROTEST MOVEMENT OPPOSING RACIAL SEGREGATION
AND DISCRIMINATION AGAINST AFRICAN AMERICANS.

1954
BROWN V. THE BOARD OF EDUCATION

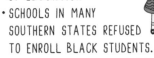

- SCHOOLS IN MANY SOUTHERN STATES REFUSED TO ENROLL BLACK STUDENTS.
- THIS LANDMARK SUPREME COURT CASE DECLARED SEGREGATION IN PUBLIC SCHOOLS TO BE UNCONSTITUTIONAL.

1955
THE MONTGOMERY BUS BOYCOTT

- POLITICAL AND SOCIAL CAMPAIGN THAT STARTED IN DECEMBER 1955 WITH THE ARREST OF **ROSA PARKS** FOR REFUSING TO GIVE HER SEAT TO A WHITE PASSENGER.
- BLACK PEOPLE WALKED, BIKED, AND HITCHHIKED INSTEAD OF TAKING THE BUS. VOLUNTEERS (BLACK AND WHITE) ORGANIZED CARPOOLING SYSTEMS.
- THE BOYCOTT LASTED 381 DAYS AND IT CREATED SERIOUS ECONOMIC DISTRESS IN MONTGOMERY BECAUSE OF THE EFFECT ON THE CITY TRANSIT SYSTEM.
- IT ENDED IN DECEMBER 1956 WITH A FEDERAL RULING DECLARING SEGREGATION ON BUSES UNCONSTITUTIONAL.

1960
THE GREENSBORO SIT-INS

- FOUR BLACK STUDENTS IN NORTH CAROLINA CAME INTO A WOOLWORTH AND SAT AT THE LUNCH COUNTER RESERVED FOR WHITE PEOPLE. WHEN THEY WERE REFUSED SERVICE THEY STAYED SEATED SILENTLY UNTIL THE STORE CLOSED.
- THEY CONTINUED THEIR QUIET PROTEST FOR WEEKS AND INSPIRED MANY STUDENTS TO DO THE SAME IN STORES IN THE SOUTHERN STATES. AS A RESULT, THE STORE REMOVED ITS POLICY OF RACIAL SEGREGATION.

1961
FREEDOM RIDERS

- BLACK AND WHITE AMERICANS PROTESTED BY RIDING TRAINS AND BUSES TOGETHER THROUGHOUT THE DEEP SOUTH.
- MANY BUSES WERE SET ON FIRE AND PROTESTORS WERE BEATEN AND ARRESTED.
- AS A RESULT, REGULATIONS WERE ISSUED PROHIBITING SEGREGATION ON BUSES AND TRAINS NATIONWIDE.

1963
THE BIRMINGHAM MOVEMENT

- MORE THAN 1,000 YOUNG STUDENTS MARCHED IN PROTEST OF SEGREGATION.
- THERE WERE 600 PHYSICAL ALTERCATIONS WITH THE POLICE, INCLUDING DOG ATTACKS.

1963
THE MARCH ON WASHINGTON FOR JOBS AND FREEDOM

- 250,000 AMERICANS OF MANY RACES STOOD UP TO THE POLITICAL AND SOCIAL INJUSTICES BLACK PEOPLE WERE FACING.
- AT THE MARCH, DR. MARTIN LUTHER KING JR. DELIVERED HIS HISTORIC "I HAVE A DREAM" SPEECH IN WHICH HE CALLED FOR AN END TO RACISM.

DR. MARTIN LUTHER KING JR.'S LEADERSHIP WAS FUNDAMENTAL IN THE FIGHT FOR CIVIL RIGHTS AND EQUALITY FOR ALL AMERICANS.

1964
THE CIVIL RIGHTS ACT OF 1964
ENDED SEGREGATION IN PUBLIC PLACES AND BANNED EMPLOYMENT DISCRIMINATION ON THE BASIS OF RACE, COLOR, RELIGION, SEX, OR NATIONAL ORIGIN.

1965
THE VOTING RIGHTS ACT OF 1965

- REMOVED MANY OF THE MECHANISMS USED TO SUPPRESS VOTING IN BLACK COMMUNITIES.
- THIS LEGISLATION WAS IN PART SPURRED ON BY THE "BLOODY SUNDAY" MARCH FROM SELMA, AL, TO MONTGOMERY, AL.

1973

ROE v. WADE

- A LANDMARK SUPREME COURT DECISION THAT ESTABLISHED A WOMAN'S LEGAL RIGHT TO AN ABORTION.
- THE COURT RULED THAT A WOMAN'S RIGHT TO CHOOSE AN ABORTION WAS PROTECTED BY THE PRIVACY RIGHTS GUARANTEED BY THE FOURTEENTH AMENDMENT TO THE U.S. CONSTITUTION.

- SEVERAL CASES THAT CAME AFTER HAVE NARROWED THE SCOPE OF ROE v. WADE BUT IT HAS NOT BEEN OVERTURNED.

2015

OBERGEFELL v. HODGES

2013 – PRESENT
BLACK LIVES MATTER MOVEMENT
#BLACKLIVESMATTER

- A POLITICAL MOVEMENT CREATED BY THREE ACTIVISTS, ALICIA GARZA, PATRISSE CULLORS, AND OPAL TOMETI IN RESPONSE TO THE ACQUITAL OF GEORGE ZIMMERMAN, TRAYVON MARTIN'S MURDERER.
- THE MOVEMENT STARTED WITH A HASHTAG IN 2013 AND BY 2016 IT HAD OVER 30 LOCAL CHAPTERS AROUND THE U.S.
- THE MOVEMENT CAMPAIGNS AGAINST POLICE BRUTALITY, RACIAL PROFILING, RACIAL INEQUALITY IN THE CRIMINAL JUSTICE SYSTEM, AND OTHER ISSUES RELATED TO VIOLENCE TOWARDS BLACK COMMUNITES.

- IN THIS CIVIL RIGHTS CASE, THE SUPREME COURT RULED THAT THE FUNDAMENTAL RIGHT TO MARRY IS GUARANTEED TO SAME-SEX COUPLES AND ALL FIFTY STATES MUST LAWFULLY PERFORM AND RECOGNIZE THESE MARRIAGES ON THE SAME TERMS AND CONDITIONS AS THE MARRIAGES OF OPPOSITE-SEX COUPLES, WITH ALL THE ACCOMPANYING RIGHTS AND RESPONSIBILITIES.
- OTHER LGBTQIA RIGHTS VARY FROM JURISDICTION TO JURISDICTION, LEAVING THEM UNPROTECTED FROM MANY TYPES OF DISCRIMINATION.

APRIL 2016 – FEBRUARY 2017
THE DAKOTA ACCESS PIPELINE MOVEMENT
#NODAPL

- A GRASSROOTS MOVEMENT THAT BEGAN IN EARLY 2016 IN REACTION TO THE APPROVED CONSTRUCTION OF THE DAKOTA ACCESS PIPELINE.
- THE STANDING ROCK SIOUX AND ALLIED ORGANIZATIONS TOOK LEGAL ACTION AIMED AT STOPPING CONSTRUCTION OF THE PROJECT. A YOUNG MEMBER OF THE COMMUNITY, TOKATA IRON EYES, AND HER FRIENDS CREATED THE HASHTAG AND SOCIAL MEDIA CAMPAIGN THAT LATER MORPHED INTO A LARGER MOVEMENT.
- THE CAMPAIGN WAS CREATED TO RAISE AWARENESS ABOUT THE THREAT OF THE PIPELINE TO SACRED BURIAL GROUNDS AS WELL AS TO THE QUALITY OF WATER IN THE AREA.
- IT HAD THE SUPPORT OF MANY NATIVE AMERICAN ORGANIZATIONS, POLITICIANS, ENVIRONMENTAL GROUPS, AND CIVIL RIGHTS GROUPS, AND THOUSANDS OF CITIZENS JOINED THE PROTESTS.
- ON JANUARY 2017, PRESIDENT DONALD TRUMP SIGNED AN EXECUTIVE ORDER ALLOWING THE PIPELINE'S CONSTRUCTION TO PROCEED.

2017

THE WOMEN'S MARCH

- A WORLDWIDE PROTEST ON JANUARY 21, 2017 TO ADVOCATE FOR LEGISLATION AND POLICIES REGARDING REPRODUCTIVE RIGHTS, LGBTQIA RIGHTS, WORKERS' RIGHTS, CIVIL RIGHTS, DISABILITY RIGHTS, IMMIGRANT RIGHTS, ENVIRONMENTAL JUSTICE, THE END OF VIOLENCE TOWARDS WOMEN, AND OTHER PROGRESSIVE RIGHTS AND PROTECTIONS.
- ONE DAY AFTER PRESIDENT DONALD TRUMP'S INNAUGURATION, AROUND 4.6 MILLION PEOPLE IN DIFFERENT CITIES IN THE U.S. AND AROUND THE WORLD JOINED THE MARCH, WHICH INITIALLY WAS SCHEDULED TO ONLY HAPPEN IN WASHINGTON, D.C.
- IT WAS THE LARGEST SINGLE-DAY DEMONSTRATION IN U.S. HISTORY.

THE UNITED STATES ARMED FORCES

IT CONSISTS OF THE ARMY, MARINE CORPS, NAVY, AND AIR FORCE, ALL UNDER THE COMMAND OF THE UNITED STATES DEPARTMENT OF DEFENSE, AND THE UNITED STATES COAST GUARD, CONTROLLED BY THE DEPARTMENT OF HOMELAND SECURITY.

THE DEFENSE BUDGET

THE UNITED STATES SPENDS FAR MORE MONEY THAN ANY OTHER COUNTRY ON DEFENSE.

2015

MILITARY EXPENDITURE IN BILLION DOLLARS

JAPAN $41 BN
FRANCE $51 BN
INDIA $51 BN
UK $55 BN
RUSSIA $66 BN
SAUDI ARABIA $87 BN

UNITED STATES
$598 BN

CHINA $215 BN

ALL MEN BETWEEN 18 AND 26 YEARS MUST REGISTER FOR THE SELECTIVE SERVICE SYSTEM.

MILITARY SEALS

MILITARY MOTTOS

THE UNITED STATES ARMY
"THIS WE'LL DEFEND"

THE UNITED STATES NAVY
"SEMPER FORTIS: ALWAYS COURAGEOUS"

THE UNITED STATES COAST GUARD
"SEMPER PARATUS: ALWAYS READY"

THE UNITED STATES AIR FORCE
"AIM HIGH: FLY–FIGHT–WIN"

THE UNITED STATES MARINE CORPS
"SEMPER FIDELIS: ALWAYS FAITHFUL"

WARS 1800-1898

1812-1815

1846-1848

WAR OF 1812

- WAR BETWEEN THE UNITED STATES AND THE UNITED KINGDOM AND THEIR RESPECTIVE ALLIES.
- PRESIDENT JAMES MADISON SIGNED THE AMERICAN DECLARATION OF WAR.
- BY 1814, NEITHER SIDE HAD ACHIEVED THEIR MAIN WAR GOALS.
- THE TREATY OF GHENT RESTORED RELATIONS BETWEEN THE TWO NATIONS.

MEXICAN-AMERICAN WAR

- AMERICA WANTED TO CONTINUE EXPANDING WEST.
- PRESIDENT POLK OFFERED MEXICO $30 MILLION FOR NEW MEXICO AND CALIFORNIA.
- MEXICO DIDN'T AGREE TO THE DEAL, SO THE UNITED STATES DECLARED WAR.
- MEXICO LOST AND SIGNED THE TREATY OF GUADALUPE HIDALGO, WHICH GAVE THE UNITED STATES OWNERSHIP OF LAND LOCATED IN ARIZONA, CALIFORNIA, WESTERN COLORADO, NEVADA, NEW MEXICO, TEXAS, AND UTAH.

MANIFEST DESTINY

A WIDELY HELD BELIEF THAT THE AMERICAN SETTLERS WERE DESTINED TO EXPAND ACROSS NORTH AMERICA. THERE WERE THREE KEY THEMES TO THIS BELIEF:

- THE VIRTUE OF THE AMERICAN PEOPLE AND THEIR INSTITUTIONS
- THE MISSION TO SPREAD THESE INSTITUTIONS
- THE DESTINY UNDER GOD TO DO THIS WORK

1861–1865

THE CIVIL WAR

- WAR BETWEEN THE UNION (ANTI-SLAVERY STATES) AND THE CONFEDERACY (PRO-SLAVERY STATES).
- AFTER FOUR YEARS OF WAR, THE NORTH (THE UNION) DEFEATED THE SOUTH.

PRESIDENT
JAMES K. POLK

VERY EAGER TO ACQUIRE MORE TERRITORY, POLK BELIEVED IN MANIFEST DESTINY.

1898 APR–AUG

SPANISH–AMERICAN WAR

- THE BIGGEST NATIONS OF THE WORLD WERE BUILDING EMPIRES, CONSISTING OF COLONIES THAT HAD BEEN CONQUERED.
- CUBA WANTED TO DECLARE INDEPENDENCE FROM SPAIN.
- THE UNITED STATES WANTED TO KEEP CUBA FROM BEING A COLONY OF SPAIN TO KEEP SPAIN FROM BECOMING TOO POWERFUL. THEY INTERVENED TO HELP CUBA.
- AFTER LOSING THE WAR AND SIGNING THE TREATY OF PARIS, SPAIN RELINQUISHED CUBA AND CEDED PUERTO RICO, GUAM, AND THE PHILLIPPINE ISLANDS TO THE UNITED STATES.

WARS 1900-1991

1914-1918

WORLD WAR I

- GERMANY, AUSTRIA-HUNGARY, BULGARIA, AND THE OTTOMAN EMPIRE (THE CENTRAL POWERS) FOUGHT AGAINST GREAT BRITAIN, FRANCE, RUSSIA, ITALY, JAPAN, ROMANIA, AND THE UNITED STATES (THE ALLIED POWERS).
- NEARLY 9 MILLION SOLDIERS WERE KILLED IN ACTION.
- CIVILIAN CASUALTIES CAUSED INDIRECTLY BY THE WAR NUMBERED CLOSE TO 10 MILLION.

PRESIDENT
WOODROW WILSON
1913-1921

AFTER THE WAR, WILSON HELPED NEGOTIATE A PEACE TREATY CALLED THE TREATY OF VERSAILLES. IN 1919 HE WAS AWARDED THE NOBEL PEACE PRIZE FOR HIS PEACE-MAKING EFFORTS.

1939-1945

WORLD WAR II

- WORLD WAR II WAS FOUGHT BETWEEN THE AXIS POWERS (GERMANY, JAPAN AND ITALY) AND THE ALLIED POWERS (BRITAIN, THE UNITED STATES, CANADA, THE SOVIET UNION, AND FRANCE).
- WWII INVOLVED MORE COUNTRIES, COST MORE MONEY, AND KILLED MORE PEOPLE THAN ANY OTHER WAR IN HUMAN HISTORY.
- AMONG THE ESTIMATED 35 TO 40 MILLION PEOPLE KILLED WERE 6 MILLION JEWS MURDERED IN NAZI CONCENTRATION CAMPS.

PRESIDENT
FRANKLIN D. ROOSEVELT
1933-1945

ELECTED IN THE EARLY YEARS OF THE GREAT DEPRESSION, FDR IS THE ONLY PRESIDENT IN AMERICAN HISTORY TO BE ELECTED FOUR TIMES; AMERICA TRUSTED HIS LEADERSHIP THROUGH THE WAR.

1947-1991

THE COLD WAR

- A STATE OF TENSION AND RIVALRY BETWEEN THE UNITED STATES AND THE SOVIET UNION.
- THE TWO SUPERPOWERS HAD FUNDAMENTAL ECONOMIC AND POLITICAL DIFFERENCES.
- ONE OF THE MAIN CONCERNS OF THE UNITED STATES WAS THE SPREAD OF COMMUNISM.
- THEY NEVER ENGAGED DIRECTLY IN FULL-SCALE ARMED COMBAT, BUT BOTH WERE HEAVILY ARMED IN PREPARATION FOR A POSSIBLE ALL-OUT NUCLEAR WORLD WAR.
- A REVOLUTIONARY WAVE SWEPT ACROSS CENTRAL AND EASTERN EUROPE IN 1989, PEACEFULLY OVERTHROWING MANY SOVIET-STYLE COMMUNIST STATES.
- IN 1991 THE SOVIET UNION WAS DISSOLVED, PUTTING AN END TO THE COLD WAR.

1950-1953

THE KOREAN WAR

- THE NORTH KOREAN ARMY (BACKED BY THE SOVIETS) INVADED SOUTH KOREA (ANTI-COMMUNIST).
- THE UNITED STATES ENTERED THE WAR ON BEHALF OF SOUTH KOREA.
- THE INVASION OF SOUTH KOREA BY THE NORTH WAS SEEN AS THE FIRST STEP IN A COMMUNIST CAMPAIGN TO TAKE OVER THE WORLD, FUELING AN ANTI-COMMUNIST HYSTERIA IN THE UNITED STATES.
- AFTER THREE YEARS OF NEGOTIATIONS BETWEEN THE UNITED STATES, NORTH KOREA, AND CHINA THE WAR ENDED.
- NEARLY 3 MILLION PEOPLE DIED. MORE THAN HALF OF THESE WERE CIVILIANS. ALMOST 40,000 AMERICAN SOLDIERS WERE KILLED IN ACTION.

WARS 1955-PRESENT

1955-1975

THE VIETNAM WAR

- LIKE KOREA, AFTER WORLD WAR II, VIETNAM HAD BEEN SPLIT INTO TWO PARTS, ONE COMMUNIST (BACKED BY THE SOVIETS) AND ONE DEMOCRATIC (BACKED BY SOUTH KOREA, AUSTRALIA, THE UNITED STATES, AND OTHERS).
- NORTH VIETNAM SOUGHT TO UNIFY THE NATION. IN 1965 THE UNITED STATES OFFICIALLY ENGAGED IN A GROUND WAR IN AN ATTEMPT TO PREVENT WHAT IT PERCEIVED WAS A COMMUNIST TAKEOVER OF SOUTH VIETNAM.
- FRAUGHT WITH CONTROVERSY AND PROTEST, THE WAR LASTED 20 YEARS AND ENDED WITH THE WITHDRAWAL OF U.S. FORCES AND THE UNIFICATION OF VIETNAM UNDER COMMUNIST CONTROL.
- MORE THAN 3 MILLION PEOPLE, INCLUDING 58,000 AMERICANS, WERE KILLED IN THE CONFLICT.

1990-1991

THE PERSIAN GULF WAR

- IRAQ INVADED NEIGHBORING KUWAIT, CLAIMING IT WAS STEALING IRAQ'S OIL.
- SAUDI ARABIA, EGYPT, AND OTHER ARAB POWERS CALLED ON THE UNITED STATES AND OTHER WESTERN NATIONS, KNOWN AS THE INTERNATIONAL COALITION, TO INTERVENE.
- THE PERSIAN GULF WAR BEGAN WITH A MASSIVE U.S.-LED AIR OFFENSIVE KNOWN AS OPERATION DESERT STORM.
- AFTER 42 DAYS OF ATTACKS, PRESIDENT GEORGE H. W. BUSH DECLARED A CEASE-FIRE. BY THAT TIME, MOST IRAQI FORCES IN KUWAIT HAD EITHER SURRENDERED OR FLED.
- INITIALLY THE PERSIAN GULF WAR WAS CONSIDERED A SUCCESS FOR THE INTERNATIONAL COALITION, BUT ONGOING CONFLICT IN THE REGION LED TO ANOTHER WAR, THE IRAQ WAR.

WAR IN AFGHANISTAN

- ON SEPTEMBER 11, 2001, MEMBERS OF THE ISLAMIC EXTREMIST GROUP AL-QAEDA CARRIED OUT SUICIDE ATTACKS AGAINST THE UNITED STATES BY FLYING TWO FULLY LOADED PASSENGER PLANES INTO THE WORLD TRADE CENTER'S TWIN TOWERS IN NEW YORK AND THE PENTAGON IN WASHINGTON, D.C. A FOURTH PLANE CRASHED IN A FIELD IN PENNSYLVANIA.
- THE UNITED STATES REQUESTED THE EXTRADITION OF AL-QAEDA'S LEADER, OSAMA BIN LADEN, BUT THE REQUEST WAS REFUSED BY THE TALIBAN, AFGHANISTAN'S EXTREMIST RULING ORGANIZATION.
- THE UNITED STATES BEGAN FIGHTING IN AFGHANISTAN IN ORDER TO DISMANTLE AL-QAEDA AND TO REMOVE THE TALIBAN FROM POWER. THE TALIBAN WERE QUICKLY DRIVEN OUT OF THE CAPITAL CITY, KABUL.
- IN 2011, OSAMA BIN LADEN WAS KILLED BY U.S. SOLDIERS DURING AN OPERATION ORDERED BY PRESIDENT BARACK OBAMA.
- THE WAR CONTINUES TODAY AND IT IS THE LONGEST "BOOTS ON THE GROUND" WAR IN THE HISTORY OF THE UNITED STATES.

THE IRAQ WAR

- CLAIMING IRAQ HAD WEAPONS OF MASS DESTRUCTION THAT ITS LEADER, SADDAM HUSSEIN, PLANNED TO USE AT ANY MOMENT, THE GEORGE W. BUSH ADMINISTRATION INVADED IRAQ WITH A COALITION OF SEVERAL OTHER ALLIED NATIONS.
- NO WEAPONS OF MASS DESTRUCTION WERE EVER FOUND, LEADING TO PROTESTS AGAINST THE WAR AROUND THE WORLD.
- THE UNITED STATES FORMALLY WITHDREW ALL COMBAT TROOPS FROM IRAQ IN 2011.

THE GROWTH OF THE UNITED STATES

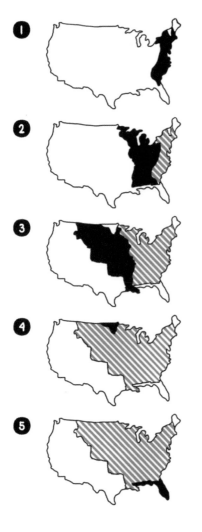

1
1620
13 ORIGINAL COLONIES

2
1783 TREATY OF PARIS
NEGOTIATED BETWEEN THE UNITED STATES AND
GREAT BRITAIN.

3
1803 LOUISIANA PURCHASE
PURCHASED FROM FRANCE FOR $15 MILLION. LAND
FROM PRESENT-DAY KANSAS, ARKANSAS, IOWA,
MISSOURI, OKLAHOMA, NORTH AND SOUTH DAKOTA,
NEBRASKA, MINNESOTA, MONTANA, NEW MEXICO,
TEXAS, WYOMING, COLORADO, AND LOUISIANA.

4
1818 RED RIVER VALLEY
THE TREATY OF 1818 BETWEEN THE UNITED
STATES AND THE UNITED KINGDOM OF GREAT
BRITAN AND IRELAND ESTABLISHED THE
OFFICIAL U.S.-CANADA BORDER.

5
1819 FLORIDA PURCHASE
ADAMS-ONÍS TREATY. PURCHASED FROM SPAIN
FOR $5 MILLION.

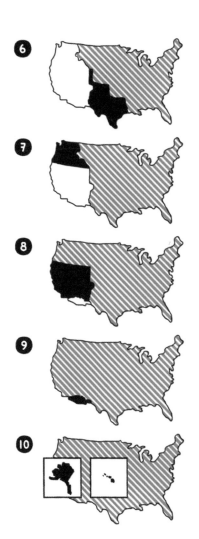

1845 ANNEXATION OF TEXAS
THE INDEPENDENT REPUBLIC OF TEXAS JOINED THE UNITED STATES AND BECAME TEXAS, THE 28TH STATE.

1846 OREGON TREATY
SIGNED BETWEEN THE UNITED STATES AND GREAT BRITAIN, THIS TREATY INCLUDED PRESENT-DAY STATES OREGON, IDAHO, WASHINGTON, AND PARTS OF MONTANA AND WYOMING.

1848 MEXICAN CESSION
CEDED AFTER THE MEXICAN-AMERICAN WAR. INCLUDED ALL OF THE PRESENT-DAY STATES OF CALIFORNIA, NEVADA, AND UTAH, AS WELL AS PARTS OF ARIZONA, COLORADO, NEW MEXICO, AND WYOMING.

1853 GADSDEN PURCHASE
PURCHASED FROM MEXICO FOR $10 MILLION. INCLUDED PRESENT-DAY SOUTHERN ARIZONA AND SOUTHWESTERN NEW MEXICO.

1867 ALASKA
PURCHASED FROM RUSSIA FOR $7.2 MILLION.

1898 HAWAIIAN ISLANDS
THE KINGDOM OF HAWAII JOINED THE UNITED STATES AND BECAME HAWAII, THE 50TH STATE, IN 1959.

U.S. TERRITORIES

PUERTO RICO

IN 1898, AFTER THE SPANISH-AMERICAN WAR, THE UNITED STATES WON CONTROL OF PUERTO RICO. IN 1917 PUERTO RICANS WERE GRANTED U.S. CITIZENSHIP.

U.S. VIRGIN ISLANDS

THE TREATY OF THE DANISH WEST INDIES WAS SIGNED IN 1916. IT TRANSFERRED SOVEREIGNTY OF THE VIRGIN ISLANDS FROM DENMARK TO THE UNITED STATES. U.S. CITIZENSHIP WAS GRANTED TO THE INHABITANTS OF THE ISLANDS IN 1927.

NORTHERN MARIANA ISLANDS

THE NORTHERN MARIANA ISLANDS ARE A SELF-GOVERNING
COMMONWEALTH IN ASSOCIATION WITH THE UNITED STATES.
IN 1986, ELIGIBLE RESIDENTS OF THE COMMONWEALTH
BECAME U.S. CITIZENS.

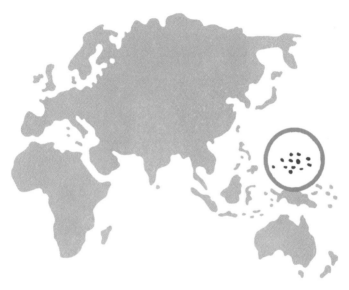

AMERICAN SAMOA

THE UNITED STATES FORMALLY
ACCEPTED THE CESSION OF
AMERICAN SAMOA IN 1929.
THE ISLAND'S CITIZENS ARE U.S.
NATIONALS (WITH THE RIGHT TO
ENTER AND RESIDE IN THE UNITED
STATES) BUT NOT CITIZENS.

GUAM

IN 1898, THE UNITED STATES
CAPTURED GUAM IN A BLOODLESS
EVENT DURING THE SPANISH-
AMERICAN WAR. IN 1952, U.S.
CITIZENSHIP WAS GRANTED TO
"ALL PERSONS BORN IN THE ISLAND
ON OR AFTER APRIL 11, 1899."

U.S. BORDERS, CITIES, RIVERS, AND OCEANS

BORDERS WITH CANADA

ALASKA
WASHINGTON
IDAHO
MONTANA
MINNESOTA
MICHIGAN
OHIO
NEW YORK
NORTH DAKOTA
PENNSYLVANIA
VERMONT
NEW HAMPSHIRE
MAINE

BORDERS WITH MEXICO

CALIFORNIA
NEW MEXICO
ARIZONA
TEXAS

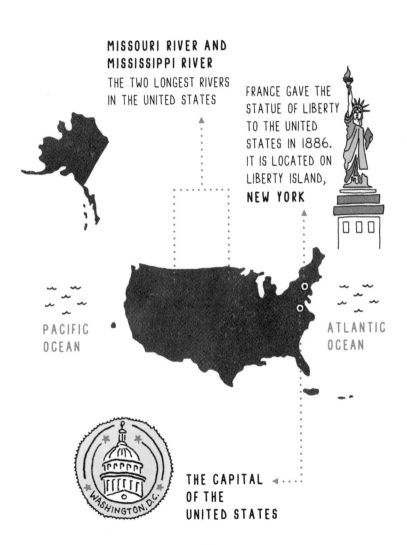

**MISSOURI RIVER AND
MISSISSIPPI RIVER**

THE TWO LONGEST RIVERS
IN THE UNITED STATES

FRANCE GAVE THE
STATUE OF LIBERTY
TO THE UNITED
STATES IN 1886.
IT IS LOCATED ON
LIBERTY ISLAND,
NEW YORK

PACIFIC
OCEAN

ATLANTIC
OCEAN

**THE CAPITAL
OF THE
UNITED STATES**

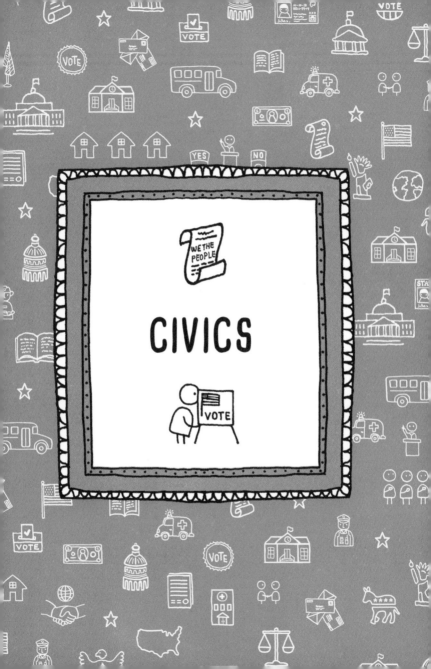

CIVICS

AMENDMENTS TO
THE BILL OF RIGHTS

FIRST AMENDMENT ——

- FREEDOM OF RELIGION
- FREEDOM OF SPEECH
- FREEDOM OF PRESS
- FREEDOM TO ASSEMBLE
- FREEDOM TO PETITION THE GOVERNMENT

SECOND AMENDMENT
RIGHT TO BEAR ARMS

THIRD AMENDMENT
NO REQUIREMENT TO HOUSE SOLDIERS

FOURTH AMENDMENT
PROTECTION FROM UNREASONABLE SEARCH AND SEIZURE

FIFTH AMENDMENT
PROTECTION OF RIGHTS TO LIFE, LIBERTY, PROPERTY, AND PROTECTION
AGAINST SELF-INCRIMINATION

SIXTH AMENDMENT
RIGHTS OF ACCUSED PERSONS IN CRIMINAL CASES

SEVENTH AMENDMENT
RIGHTS IN CIVIL CASES

EIGHTH AMENDMENT
EXCESSIVE BAIL, FINES, AND PUNISHMENTS FORBIDDEN

NINTH AMENDMENT
RIGHTS OF CITIZENS CANNOT BE LIMITED BY THOSE LISTED IN THE CONSTITUTION

TENTH AMENDMENT
UNDELEGATED POWERS KEPT BY THE STATES AND THE PEOPLE

FIRST AMENDMENT:
FREEDOM OF RELIGION

47

FIRST AMENDMENT:
FREEDOM OF SPEECH

FIRST AMENDMENT:
FREEDOM OF PRESS

FIRST AMENDMENT:
FREEDOM OF ASSEMBLY

FIRST AMENDMENT:
FREEDOM TO PETITION THE GOVERNMENT

SECOND AMENDMENT:
RIGHT TO BEAR ARMS

THIRD AMENDMENT:
NO REQUIREMENT TO HOUSE SOLDIERS

FOURTH AMENDMENT:
PROTECTION FROM UNREASONABLE SEARCHES AND SEIZURES

FIFTH AMENDMENT:
PROTECTION OF RIGHTS TO LIFE, LIBERTY, AND PROPERTY
AND PROTECTION AGAINST SELF-INCRIMINATION

SIXTH AMENDMENT:
RIGHTS OF ACCUSED PERSONS IN CRIMINAL CASES

SEVENTH AMENDMENT:
RIGHTS IN CIVIL CASES

EIGHTH AMENDMENT
EXCESSIVE BAIL, FINES, AND PUNISHMENTS FORBIDDEN

NINTH AMENDMENT:
RIGHTS OF CITIZENS CANNOT BE LIMITED
BY THOSE LISTED IN THE CONSTITUTION

TENTH AMENDMENT:
UNDELEGATED POWERS KEPT BY THE STATES AND THE PEOPLE

FOUR AMENDMENTS ABOUT VOTING

THE 15TH AMENDMENT

1870

OUTLAWED DISCRIMINATION IN
VOTING RIGHTS, GRANTING
(ON PAPER) AFRICAN-AMERICAN
MEN THE RIGHT TO VOTE.
DESPITE THE AMENDMENT, THERE
WERE VARIOUS DISCRIMINATORY
PRACTICES USED TO PREVENT
BLACK MEN FROM VOTING.

THE 19TH AMENDMENT

1919

GRANTED AMERICAN WOMEN
THE RIGHT TO VOTE.
ELIZABETH CADY STANTON,
LUCRETIA MOTT, AND
SUSAN B. ANTHONY WERE THREE
IMPORTANT ACTIVISTS BEHIND
THE WOMEN'S RIGHTS MOVEMENT
AND WOMEN'S SUFFRAGE.

THE 24TH AMENDMENT

1964

PROHIBITED BOTH CONGRESS
AND THE STATES FROM
INTERFERING WITH THE RIGHT
TO VOTE IN FEDERAL ELECTIONS
BY USING ANY TYPE OF TAX.
POLL TAXES, GRANDFATHER
CLAUSES, AND INTIMIDATION
PREVENTED AFRICAN-AMERICANS
FROM VOTING.

THE 26TH AMENDMENT

1971

LOWERED THE VOTING AGE FROM
21 TO 18. IT WAS DRIVEN IN
LARGE PART BY THE BROADER
STUDENT ACTIVISM MOVEMENT
PROTESTING THE VIETNAM WAR,
DRAWING ATTENTION TO THE
HYPOCRISY OF DRAFTING YOUNG
PEOPLE WHO LACKED THE RIGHT
TO VOTE.

BRANCHES AND PARTS OF THE GOVERNMENT

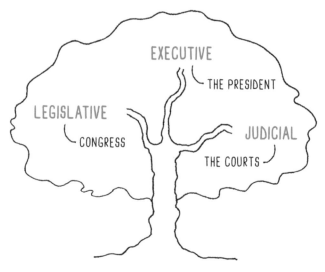

EXECUTIVE
THE PRESIDENT
LEGISLATIVE
CONGRESS
JUDICIAL
THE COURTS

ONE BRANCH OF THE GOVERNMENT CAN'T
BECOME TOO POWERFUL BECAUSE OF

SEPARATION OF POWERS CHECKS AND BALANCES

THE FOUNDING FATHERS, CONCERNED WITH CENTRALIZED POWER, CREATED
THREE DIFFERENT BRANCHES OF GOVERNMENT TO ADMINISTER THREE DIFFERENT
TYPES OF POWER. EACH BRANCH HAS CHECKS AND BALANCES OVER THE
OTHER TWO.

CHECKS AND BALANCES

THE PRESIDENT CAN SIGN
OR VETO LAWS PASSED
BY CONGRESS.

CONGRESS CAN CONFIRM
OR REJECT THE PRESIDENT'S
APPOINTMENTS, IT CAN
OVERRIDE A PRESIDENT'S VETO,
AND IT CAN REMOVE THE
PRESIDENT FROM OFFICE IN
EXCEPTIONAL CIRCUMSTANCES.

THE JUSTICES OF THE SUPREME
COURT ARE NOMINATED BY THE
PRESIDENT AND CONGRESS HAS
THE POWER TO APPROVE OR REJECT
THE NOMINATION. THE JUSTICES
CAN OVERTURN UNCONSTITUTIONAL
LAWS AND DECLARE THE PRESIDENT'S
ORDERS UNCONSTITUTIONAL.

THE EXECUTIVE BRANCH

THE EXECUTIVE BRANCH CARRIES OUT
THE LAWS MADE BY CONGRESS.

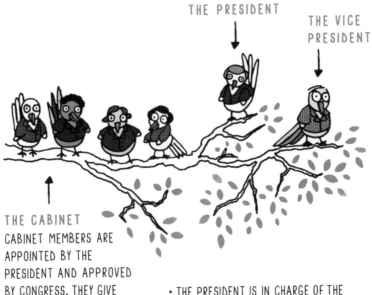

THE PRESIDENT

THE VICE
PRESIDENT

THE CABINET
CABINET MEMBERS ARE
APPOINTED BY THE
PRESIDENT AND APPROVED
BY CONGRESS. THEY GIVE
ADVICE TO THE PRESIDENT.

- THE PRESIDENT IS IN CHARGE OF THE
  EXECUTIVE BRANCH.
- SHE/HE IS ELECTED FOR FOUR YEARS.
- SHE/HE SIGNS BILLS INTO LAW AND HAS
  THE POWER TO VETO BILLS.
- THE PRESIDENT IS THE COMMANDER IN
  CHIEF OF THE MILITARY.

CABINET POSITIONS

VICE PRESIDENT

SECRETARY OF

ATTORNEY GENERAL

AGRICULTURE

COMMERCE

DEFENSE

TRANSPORTATION

ENERGY

EDUCATION

VETERANS AFFAIRS

THE INTERIOR

LABOR

STATE

HEALTH + HUMAN SERVICES

THE TREASURY

HOMELAND SECURITY

HOUSING + URBAN DEVELOPMENT

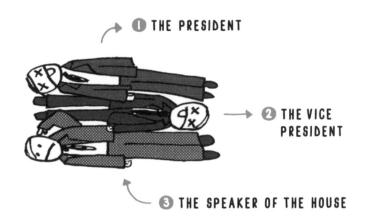

→ **1 THE PRESIDENT**

→ **2 THE VICE PRESIDENT**

↖ **3 THE SPEAKER OF THE HOUSE**

EVERY FOUR YEARS, ON THE FIRST TUESDAY OF NOVEMBER, WE VOTE TO ELECT THE PRESIDENT. I AM THANKFUL FOR DEMOCRACY AND VEGETARIANISM.

PRESIDENTS OF THE UNITED STATES

1
GEORGE WASHINGTON
1789-1797

2
JOHN ADAMS
1797-1801

3
THOMAS JEFFERSON
1801-1809

4
JAMES MADISON
1809-1817

5
JAMES MONROE
1817-1825

6
JOHN QUINCY ADAMS
1825-1829

7
ANDREW JACKSON
1829-1837

8
MARTIN VAN BUREN
1837-1841

9
WILLIAM HENRY HARRISON
1841-1841

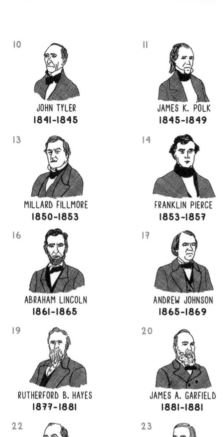

10
JOHN TYLER
1841-1845

11
JAMES K. POLK
1845-1849

12
ZACHARY TAYLOR
1849-1850

13
MILLARD FILLMORE
1850-1853

14
FRANKLIN PIERCE
1853-1857

15
JAMES BUCHANAN
1857-1861

16
ABRAHAM LINCOLN
1861-1865

17
ANDREW JOHNSON
1865-1869

18
ULYSSES S. GRANT
1869-1877

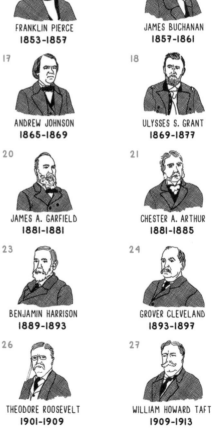

19
RUTHERFORD B. HAYES
1877-1881

20
JAMES A. GARFIELD
1881-1881

21
CHESTER A. ARTHUR
1881-1885

22
GROVER CLEVELAND
1885-1889

23
BENJAMIN HARRISON
1889-1893

24
GROVER CLEVELAND
1893-1897

25
WILLIAM MCKINLEY
1897-1901

26
THEODORE ROOSEVELT
1901-1909

27
WILLIAM HOWARD TAFT
1909-1913

28

WOODROW WILSON
1913-1921

29

WARREN G. HARDING
1921-1923

30

CALVIN COOLIDGE
1923-1929

31

HERBERT HOOVER
1929-1933

32

FRANKLIN D. ROOSEVELT
1933-1945

33

HARRY S. TRUMAN
1945-1953

34

DWIGHT D. EISENHOWER
1953-1961

35

JOHN F. KENNEDY
1961-1963

36

LYNDON B. JOHNSON
1963-1969

37

RICHARD M. NIXON
1969-1974

38

GERALD R. FORD
1974-1977

39

JIMMY CARTER
1977-1981

40

RONALD REAGAN
1981-1989

41

GEORGE H. W. BUSH
1989-1993

42

BILL CLINTON
1993-2001

43

GEORGE W. BUSH
2001-2009

44

BARACK OBAMA
2009-2017

45

DONALD J. TRUMP
2017-INCUMBENT

THE LEGISLATIVE BRANCH

THE LEGISLATIVE BRANCH ENACTS LEGISLATION
(LAWS), CONFIRMS OR REJECTS PRESIDENTIAL APPOINTMENTS,
AND HAS THE AUTHORITY TO DECLARE WAR.

IT INCLUDES CONGRESS (THE SENATE AND THE HOUSE OF
REPRESENTATIVES) AND AGENCIES THAT PROVIDE SUPPORT
TO CONGRESS.

AMERICAN CITIZENS HAVE THE RIGHT TO VOTE FOR
SENATORS AND REPRESENTATIVES.

THE FEDERAL LAWS ARE

MADE BY CONGRESS

CONGRESS

SENATE

100
SENATORS

EACH STATE GETS TWO
SENATORS. THEY
REPRESENT ALL THE
PEOPLE OF THEIR STATE

ELECTED FOR
SIX
YEARS

HOUSE OF REPRESENTATIVES

435
VOTING MEMBERS

THE AMOUNT OF
REPRESENTATIVES PER
STATE IS BASED ON THE
STATE'S POPULATION

ELECTED FOR
TWO
YEARS

HOW A BILL BECOMES A LAW

1

THE BILL STARTS AS AN IDEA.
A DOCUMENT IS DRAFTED TO
EXPLAIN THE PURPOSE OF THE BILL.
THIS DOCUMENT CAN BE DRAFTED BY:

MEMBERS OF CONGRESS
THE EXECUTIVE BRANCH
AN OUTSIDE GROUP

2

THE BILL CAN ONLY BE INTRODUCED
BY A MEMBER OF CONGRESS IN EITHER
OF THE TWO HOUSES OF CONGRESS.
IN THIS EXAMPLE THE BILL IS
INTRODUCED IN THE HOUSE OF
REPRESENTATIVES FIRST. IF IT WAS
INTRODUCED IN THE SENATE THE
PROCESS WOULD BE FLIPPED.

3

THE BILL GOES TO COMMITTEE.
MEMBERS RESEARCH, DISCUSS, AND
MAKE CHANGES TO THE BILL. THE
BILL CAN BE ACCEPTED, SENT TO
A SUBCOMMITTEE FOR FURTHER
RESEARCH, OR REJECTED.

HOUSE OF REPRESENTATIVES

4

THE HOUSE DEBATES THE BILL
AND MAY ADD AMENDMENTS BEFORE
VOTING. IF THE MAJORITY VOTES
FOR THE BILL, IT WILL GO TO THE
OTHER HOUSE OF CONGRESS. IN THIS
CASE, THE SENATE.

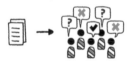

THE COMMITTEE CAN:

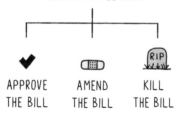

APPROVE   AMEND   KILL
THE BILL   THE BILL   THE BILL

5

A SENATOR INTRODUCES THE BILL, WHICH IS THEN SENT TO COMMITTEE. JUST LIKE IN THE OTHER HOUSE OF CONGRESS, SENATORS CAN KILL, AMEND, OR APPROVE THE BILL.

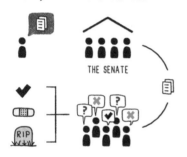

6

THE SENATE DEBATES THE BILL. AMENDMENTS MAY BE ADDED. IF A MAJORITY VOTES IN FAVOR, THE BILL IS RETURNED TO THE HOUSE OF REPRESENTATIVES FOR FINAL APPROVAL.

7

BOTH HOUSES OF CONGRESS HAVE TO AGREE ON THE SAME VERSION OF THE FINAL BILL. IF THE COMMITTEE REACHES A COMPROMISE THE BILL GOES TO THE PRESIDENT.

8

IF THE PRESIDENT APPROVES IT, THE BILL BECOMES A LAW. IF THE PRESIDENT VETOES THE BILL, IT STILL HAS A CHANCE TO BECOME A LAW IF TWO THIRDS OF EACH HOUSE VOTE TO OVERRIDE THE PRESIDENTIAL VETO.

THE JUDICIAL BRANCH

- REVIEWS LAWS
- INTERPRETS THE MEANING OF LAWS
- APPLIES LAWS TO INDIVIDUAL CASES
- DECIDES IF LAWS VIOLATE THE CONSTITUTION

IT'S COMPRISED OF THE SUPREME COURT AND OTHER FEDERAL COURTS.

THE SUPREME COURT

- IS THE HIGHEST COURT IN THE UNITED STATES.
- THE COURT CONSISTS OF THE CHIEF JUSTICE AND EIGHT ASSOCIATE JUSTICES.
- JUSTICES ARE NOMINATED BY THE PRESIDENT AND MUST BE APPROVED BY THE SENATE.
- THEY ARE APPOINTED FOR LIFE, THOUGH THEY MAY RESIGN OR RETIRE. THEY SERVE AN AVERAGE OF 16 YEARS.

THERE ARE JUSTICES 9 ON THE SUPREME COURT

RULE OF LAW

NO ONE IS ABOVE THE LAW
EVERYONE MUST OBEY THE LAW

NO ONE

THE LAW

YOU AND EVERYONE ELSE

PEOPLE YOU SHOULD KNOW

PRESIDENT

VICE PRESIDENT

SPEAKER OF THE HOUSE

POLITICAL PARTY
CURRENTLY IN THE MAJORITY

CHIEF JUSTICE OF THE U.S.
SUPREME COURT

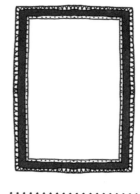

YOUR U.S REPRESENTATIVE

SENATOR OF YOUR STATE

SENATOR OF YOUR STATE

CAPITAL OF YOUR STATE

GOVERNOR OF YOUR STATE

FEDERALISM

IN THE UNITED STATES, THE POWER OF THE GOVERNMENT IS DIVIDED BETWEEN THE GOVERNMENT OF THE UNITED STATES (THE FEDERAL GOVERNMENT) AND THE GOVERNMENTS OF THE INDIVIDUAL STATES (THE STATE GOVERNMENT).

1788–1937

DUAL FEDERALISM

THE POWERS WERE STRICTLY DIVIDED BETWEEN THE NATIONAL AND STATE GOVERNMENTS. DUAL FEDERALISM IS ALSO KNOWN AS LAYER CAKE FEDERALISM.

1937–PRESENT

COOPERATIVE FEDERALISM

IN COOPERATIVE FEDERALISM, THE NATIONAL GOVERNMENT ENCOURAGES STATES AND LOCALITIES TO PURSUE NATIONALLY DEFINED GOALS. IN THIS STYLE OF FEDERALISM, POWER IS MIXED. IT'S ALSO CALLED MARBLE CAKE FEDERALISM.

GRANT-IN AID
(ENCOURAGEMENT)

NATIONAL GOVERNMENT

STATE GOVERNMENT

THE NATIONAL GOVERNMENT GIVES MONEY TO THE STATE GOVERNMENTS TO BE USED FOR SPECIFIC PURPOSES LIKE EDUCATION AND TRANSPORTATION.

IN COOPERATIVE FEDERALISM, THE NATIONAL GOVERNMENT CAN ALSO SET UP RULES AND REGULATIONS THAT STATES MUST FOLLOW. IN THESE CASES, GRANTS MAY OR MAY NOT BE GIVEN.

NATIONAL GOVERNMENT

RULES AND REGULATIONS

STATE GOVERNMENT

GOVERNMENT RESPONSIBILITIES

THESE ARE SOME OF THE RESPONSIBILITIES OF THE STATE GOVERNMENT
AND THE FEDERAL GOVERNMENT

STATE AND LOCAL GOVERNMENT	FEDERAL GOVERNMENT

PARKS & RECREATION	PUBLIC SCHOOLS & LIBRARIES	STATE LAND & ANIMAL PROTECTION	PRINT MONEY	MAKE LAWS

POLICE & FIRE DEPARTMENTS	PUBLIC WORKS	ROADS & HIGHWAYS	MAKE TREATIES	POSTAL SERVICE

PUBLIC TRANSPORTATION	PET LICENSES	DRIVER'S LICENSES & LICENSE PLATES	DECLARE WAR & ESTABLISH AN ARMY AND NAVY

RIGHTS
FOR EVERYONE
LIVING IN THE
UNITED STATES.

- FREEDOM OF EXPRESSION
- FREEDOM OF WORSHIP
- FREEDOM OF SPEECH
- FREEDOM OF ASSEMBLY
- THE RIGHT TO BEAR ARMS
- FREEDOM TO PETITION
  THE GOVERNMENT

FOR
CITIZENS OF THE
UNITED STATES
ONLY

HIGH FIVE

RIGHTS

- RUN FOR
  FEDERAL OFFICE
- VOTE FOR FEDERAL
  AND LOCAL OFFICE

RESPONSIBILITIES

- SERVE ON JURY
- VOTE FOR FEDERAL
  AND LOCAL OFFICE

THE LAST DAY
TO SEND FEDERAL
INCOME TAX
FORMS IS:

APRIL
15

- TAXES ARE MONEY COLLECTED
  BY THE GOVERNMENT TO PAY FOR
  THINGS IT DOES. IN THE UNITED
  STATES THERE ARE STATE AND
  FEDERAL TAXES.
- TAXES ARE IMPOSED ON INCOME,
  PAYROLL, PROPERTY, SALES,
  DIVIDENDS, IMPORTS, CAPITAL
  GAINS, ESTATES, AND GIFTS.

THE ECONOMIC SYSTEM OF THE UNITED STATES IS CALLED CAPITALISM OR MARKET ECONOMY. IN THIS SYSTEM, THE CAPITAL GOODS ARE PRIVATELY OWNED, THE INVESTMENTS ARE DETERMINED BY PRIVATE DECISION, AND THE PRICES, PRODUCTION, AND DISTRIBUTION OF GOODS ARE DETERMINED MAINLY BY COMPETITION IN A FREE MARKET.

HOW DO AMERICANS PARTICIPATE IN THEIR DEMOCRACY?

THE DONKEY
AND THE ELEPHANT

THE
DEMOCRATIC
PARTY

THE
REPUBLICAN
PARTY

THE TWO MAJOR POLITICAL PARTIES OF THE UNITED STATES

- IN 1824 ANDREW JACKSON RAN FOR PRESIDENT AND LOST. HE WAS SO ANGRY HE DECIDED TO CREATE HIS OWN PARTY AND TRY AGAIN. HE CALLED IT THE DEMOCRATIC PARTY.
- HIS OPPONENTS NICKNAMED HIM ANDREW JACKASS. JACKSON, RATHER THAN REJECTING THE LABEL, EMBRACED IT AND INCLUDED A DONKEY AS A MASCOT ON HIS CAMPAIGN POSTERS.
- IN 1829 ANDREW JACKSON RAN AGAIN. THIS TIME HE WON AND BECAME THE FIRST DEMOCRATIC PRESIDENT.

THOMAS NAST, CARTOONIST

- HELPED POPULARIZE THE DONKEY AS A SYMBOL FOR THE DEMOCRATIC PARTY AND CREATED THE GOP ELEPHANT.
- HE ALSO CREATED THE MODERN IMAGE OF SANTA CLAUS.

- IN 1854 THE REPUBLICAN PARTY WAS FORMED.
- IN 1861 ABRAHAM LINCOLN BECAME THE FIRST REPUBLICAN PRESIDENT.
- THE TERM GRAND OLD PARTY (GOP) ORIGINATED IN THE CONGRESSIONAL RECORD IN 1875.
- THOMAS NAST WAS RESPONSIBLE FOR INTRODUCING THE ELEPHANT AS A REPUBLICAN SYMBOL. HE USED IT IN A 1874 *HARPER'S WEEKLY* CARTOON.

CONGRESSIONAL AND MIDTERM ELECTIONS

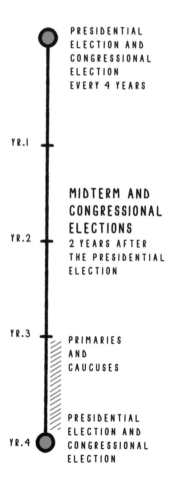

PRESIDENTIAL
ELECTION AND
CONGRESSIONAL
ELECTION
EVERY 4 YEARS

YR.1

MIDTERM AND
CONGRESSIONAL
ELECTIONS
2 YEARS AFTER
THE PRESIDENTIAL
ELECTION

YR.2

YR.3

PRIMARIES
AND
CAUCUSES

PRESIDENTIAL
ELECTION AND
CONGRESSIONAL
ELECTION

YR.4

- MIDTERM ELECTIONS HAVE A LOW VOTER TURNOUT. ONLY 40 PERCENT OF THE PEOPLE WHO PARTICIPATE IN THE GENERAL ELECTION ALSO VOTE IN THE MIDTERM ELECTIONS.
- THOSE THAT VOTE ARE MOTIVATED PARTISANS OR DRIVEN BY IDEOLOGY.

 CONGRESS

- DURING THE MIDTERMS WE VOTE TO ELECT THE MEMBERS OF CONGRESS FOR OUR STATE.
- WE ELECT ONE THIRD OF THE TOTAL NUMBER OF SENATORS AND ALL 435 MEMBERS OF THE HOUSE OF REPRESENTATIVES.
- SENATORS ARE ELECTED EVERY SIX YEARS WHILE REPRESENTATIVES ARE ELECTED EVERY TWO YEARS.
- IT IS THE ONLY BRANCH OF THE FEDERAL GOVERMENT THAT HAS DIRECT ELECTIONS.

MEMBERS OF CONGRESS, GOVERNORS, AND OTHER STATE AND LOCAL OFFICIALS ARE ELECTED THROUGH DIRECT ELECTION. UNLIKE THE PRESIDENTIAL ELECTION, IN THE MIDTERM ELECTIONS YOUR VOTE GOES DIRECTLY TO THE OFFICIAL YOU SUPPORT, NOT TO A DELEGATE OR ELECTOR.

WE SHOULD GET INVOLVED IN LOCAL POLITICS BECAUSE

LOCAL POLICIES INFLUENCE STATE POLICIES, AND STATE POLICIES INFLUENCE FEDERAL POLICIES.

MANY BIG REFORMS HAVE STARTED AS GRASSROOTS PROJECTS.

GOVERNOR

- THE GOVERNOR IS THE HEAD OF THE STATE.
- 36 STATES ELECT GOVERNORS DURING MIDTERM ELECTIONS.
- SOME OF HER/HIS DUTIES ARE TO DEVELOP THE STATE BUDGET, SIGN AND VETO STATE LAWS, MANAGE THE STATE GOVERNMENT, AND APPOINT STATE OFFICIALS, INCLUDING STATE JUDGES.

STATE LEGISLATURE

- IT HAS THE SAME GENERAL STRUCTURE AS CONGRESS, THOUGH THERE ARE A FEW EXCEPTIONS.
- LEGISLATORS REVIEW, APPROVE, AND REJECT STATE LAWS.
- THEY ALSO APPROVE THE STATE'S BUDGETS.

MUNICIPAL OFFICIALS

- STATES ARE DIVIDED IN SEVERAL WAYS: COUNTIES, BOROUGHS OR PARISHES, AND MUNICIPALITIES (CITIES AND TOWNS).
- MUNICIPAL OFFICIALS MAKE DECISIONS THAT AFFECT THE EVERYDAY LIVES OF THEIR CITIZENS.

STATE AND LOCAL ELECTIONS

LOCAL GOVERNMENT POLICIES HAVE
A BIG AND IMMEDIATE EFFECT
ON OUR EVERYDAY LIVES. HIGHER
VOTER TURNOUT IS ESSENTIAL IN
BUILDING BETTER COMMUNITIES.

THESE ARE SOME OF THE SERVICES
THAT CAN BE IMPACTED EVERY
TIME YOU CHOOSE NOT TO VOTE IN
LOCAL ELECTIONS.

BUSINESS DEVELOPMENT

EMERGENCY SERVICES

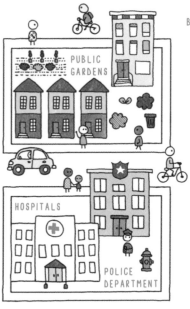

PUBLIC GARDENS

HOSPITALS

POLICE DEPARTMENT

PUBLIC HOUSING

THE ELECTORAL PROCESS
PRIMARIES AND CAUCUSES

PRIMARIES AND CAUCUSES ARE PROCESSES TO ELECT THE PRESIDENTIAL CANDIDATES FOR EACH PARTY. BOTH PRIMARIES AND CAUCUSES ARE RUN AT THE STATE LEVEL.

PRIMARIES

CAUCUSES

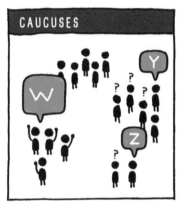

- PRIMARIES ARE STATEWIDE, ORGANIZED BY THE STATE GOVERNMENT.
- VOTERS IN EACH PARTY CAST SECRET BALLOTS FOR THE CANDIDATE THEY WANT THEIR PARTY TO SUPPORT.

- CAUCUSES ARE LOCAL GATHERINGS, ORGANIZED BY STATE PARTY OFFICIALS, WHERE VOTERS DECIDE WHO THEY WILL SUPPORT.
- VOTERS GATHER IN GROUPS AND VOTING IS OFTEN DONE BY RAISING HANDS.
- THE IOWA CAUCUS, ALWAYS HELD FIRST, MARKS THE BEGINNING OF THE ELECTION YEAR.

PRIMARIES AND CAUCUSES ARE
INDIRECT ELECTIONS

CITIZENS VOTE TO ELECT DELEGATES →
WHO ARE BOUND TO A PARTICULAR CANDIDATE.
DELEGATES REPRESENT THEIR STATES AT
THE NATIONAL PARTY CONVENTIONS, WHERE A
CEREMONIAL VOTE IS TAKEN. THE CANDIDATE
WHO RECEIVES A MAJORITY OF HIS OR HER
PARTY'S DELEGATES WINS THE NOMINATION.

CANDIDATE Z	CANDIDATE W	CANDIDATE Y
8 DELEGATES	4 DELEGATES	6 DELEGATES

NATIONAL CONVENTIONS

JUL	AUG	SEPT

DURING THE NATIONAL CONVENTIONS, EACH
PARTY ANNOUNCES THEIR PRESIDENTIAL
AND VICE PRESIDENTIAL NOMINEES.
THE NATIONAL CONVENTIONS TYPICALLY
CONFIRM THE CANDIDATE WHO HAS
ALREADY WON THE REQUIRED NUMBER OF
DELEGATES THROUGH THE PRIMARIES AND
CAUCUSES. HOWEVER, IF NO CANDIDATE HAS
RECEIVED THE MAJORITY OF A PARTY'S
DELEGATES, THE CONVENTION BECOMES THE
STAGE FOR CHOOSING THAT PARTY'S
PRESIDENTIAL NOMINEE.

THE CAMPAIGN

OCT   NOV

EACH PARTY'S CANDIDATE TRAVELS AROUND THE
COUNTRY, SHARING THEIR PLANS AND VIEWS.
DEBATES, RALLIES, ADVERTISING, AND FUNDRAISING
ARE PART OF THE PROCESS OF CAMPAIGNING.
CAMPAIGNS CAN START A YEAR OR MORE BEFORE
ELECTION DAY.

THE BEST

ELECTION DAY

NOV

ELECTION DAY IS
THE TUESDAY AFTER
THE FIRST MONDAY
IN THE MONTH
OF NOVEMBER.
VOTER TURNOUT FOR
PRESIDENTAL ELECTIONS
IN 2016 WAS ABOUT
55 PERCENT OF THE U.S.
VOTING-AGE POPULATION
(VAP). THIS IS LOW
COMPARED TO MANY
DEMOCRACTIC COUNTRIES.
MANY VOTERS ARE
NOT PARTISAN OR
IDEOLOGICALLY INCLINED.

THE ELECTORAL COLLEGE

WHEN YOU VOTE IN THE PRESIDENTIAL
ELECTION, YOU ARE VOTING FOR ELECTORS
WHO ARE PLEDGED TO VOTE FOR YOUR
CANDIDATE. THE FOUNDING FATHERS
ESTABLISHED IT IN THE CONSTITUTION AS A
COMPROMISE BETWEEN ELECTION OF THE
PRESIDENT BY A VOTE IN CONGRESS AND
ELECTION OF THE PRESIDENT BY A POPULAR
VOTE OF QUALIFIED CITIZENS.

ELECTORS

THE NUMBER OF ELECTORS PER STATE
IS DETERMINED BY THE POPULATION OF
THE STATE.

 # OF DISTRICTS OF THE STATE
+ 2 SENATORS PER STATE
_____
 # OF ELECTORS PER STATE

TOTAL
NUMBER OF
ELECTORS
IN THE UNITED
STATES: 538

IL
20
ELECTORS

CANDIDATE Y

8

CANDIDATE Z

12

IN MOST STATES, THE WINNER TAKES IT ALL. IF A CANDIDATE WINS A SIMPLE MAJORITY OF THAT STATE'S VOTES, ALL OF THE ELECTORS OF THAT STATE ARE PLEDGED TO VOTE FOR HIM OR HER.

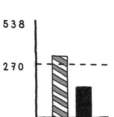

538

270

A CANDIDATE NEEDS MORE THAN HALF OF ELECTORS TO WIN THE ELECTION

270 IS THE "MAGIC NUMBER"

PARTY Z WINS ILLINOIS WITH A TOTAL OF 20 ELECTORS.

INAUGURATION DAY

ON JANUARY 20, THE PRESIDENT AND VICE PRESIDENT ARE SWORN IN AT THE U.S. CAPITOL BUILDING IN WASHINGTON, D.C.

HOW TO GET INVOLVED

REGISTER TO VOTE

. . . .

DO IT EARLY!

REREGISTRATION IS REQUIRED IF YOUR NAME OR ADDRESS CHANGES

. . . .

. . . .

YOU MUST BE 18 YEARS OR OLDER TO VOTE IN A U.S. ELECTION.

FIND OUT
IF YOUR STATE'S CAUCUSES AND PRIMARIES ARE:

OPEN

ALL REGISTERED VOTERS CAN PARTICIPATE

YOU ARE GOOD TO GO!

CLOSED

ONLY
REGISTERED
MEMBERS
OF THE PARTY CAN
PARTICIPATE

REGISTER
TO BE A MEMBER OF YOUR PARTY

3

SHOW UP
VOTE!
AND VOICE
YOUR OPINION

. . . .

PARTICIPATE AND
VOTE IN CAUCUSES,
PRIMARIES, AND THE
PRESIDENTIAL
ELECTIONS

. . . .

IF YOU ARE
GOING TO A
CAUCUS,
BE PUNCTUAL

LOBBYING

WHAT IS IT?

- IT'S THE RIGHT TO SPEAK FREELY, TO IMPACT DECISIONS, AND TO PETITION THE GOVERNMENT.
- LOBBYISTS INFLUENCE LEGISLATION, REGULATION, AND OTHER GOVERNMENT DECISIONS, ACTIONS, AND POLICIES ON BEHALF OF A GROUP OR INDIVIDUAL.
- LOBBYISTS ARE ONE OF THE MOST POLITICALLY INFLUENTIAL GROUPS. THEY CAN GET BILLS PASSED, PROGRAMS FUNDED, AND POLITICIANS ELECTED.

WHO ARE LOBBYISTS?

- IN MANY CASES LOBBYISTS ARE PEOPLE WITH PREVIOUS EXPERIENCE IN GOVERNMENT. KNOWLEDGE OF HOW THE GOVERNMENT WORKS AND INFLUENTIAL CONTACTS AND CONNECTIONS ARE VERY USEFUL FOR LOBBYING.
- LOBBYISTS CAN BE PEOPLE OR GROUPS PETITIONING THEIR REPRESENTATIVES TO VOTE FOR ISSUES THEY CARE ABOUT.
- LOBBYISTS CAN ALSO BE VERY POWERFUL COMPANIES HIRED BY CORPORATIONS TO LOBBY ON THEIR BEHALF.

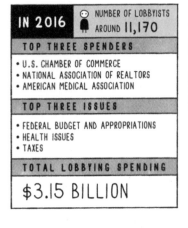

IN 2016 — NUMBER OF LOBBYISTS AROUND 11,170

TOP THREE SPENDERS
- U.S. CHAMBER OF COMMERCE
- NATIONAL ASSOCIATION OF REALTORS
- AMERICAN MEDICAL ASSOCIATION

TOP THREE ISSUES
- FEDERAL BUDGET AND APPROPRIATIONS
- HEALTH ISSUES
- TAXES

TOTAL LOBBYING SPENDING

$3.15 BILLION

LOBBYING ON BEHALF OF →

LOBBYING ON BEHALF OF →

LOBBYING FOR THE PEOPLE

MANY LOBBYISTS BUILD SUPPORT
IN CONGRESS FOR INITIATIVES
THAT ARE BENEFICIAL TO ALL
PEOPLE, LIKE AIDS PREVENTION,
CHILD SURVIVAL, POVERTY RELIEF,
CLIMATE ISSUES, MICROFINANCE,
EDUCATION, DISABILITY ISSUES,
HEALTH, AND WORKERS' BENEFITS.

55%
OF PEOPLE INTERVIEWED BY GALLUP
BELIEVE LOBBYISTS HAVE A LOT OF
INFLUENCE ON HOW CONGRESS VOTES.

ONLY 7%
OF PEOPLE INTERVIEWED RATE
LOBBYING AS A HIGHLY HONEST
AND ETHICAL PROFESSION.

FOREIGN LOBBYING

BECAUSE OF GLOBALIZATION AND
THE INFLUENCE AMERICAN POLICIES
CAN HAVE OVER OTHER COUNTRIES,
FOREIGN COMPANIES AND
GOVERNMENTS ALSO LOBBY
IN WASHINGTON.

LOBBYING FOR
PRIVATE ENTERPRISE

- PROFESSIONAL LOBBYING
COMPANIES MAKE A LOT OF MONEY
WHEN ADVOCATING FOR THEIR
CLIENTS' ISSUES.

- CORPORATIONS ARE WILLING TO
SPEND BIG SUMS OF MONEY ON
LOBBYING BECAUSE IT IS AN
INVESTMENT THAT CAN YIELD A
GREAT RETURN.

- AN EXAMPLE OF VERY SUCCESSFUL
LOBBYING TOOK PLACE FOR THE
"AMERICAN JOBS CREATION ACT."
SEVERAL CORPORATIONS HIRED A
HIGH-POWERED LOBBYING FIRM TO
SPONSOR A BILL THAT CREATED A
ONE-TIME TAX REDUCTION FOR
MULTINATIONAL FIRMS. THE
CORPORATE TAX WENT FROM 35%
TO 5%. FOR EVERY DOLLAR THE
CORPORATIONS INVESTED IN
LOBBYING FOR THIS LAW THEY GOT
$220 IN TAX BENEFITS.

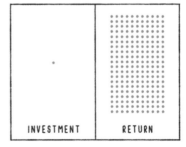

INVESTMENT | RETURN

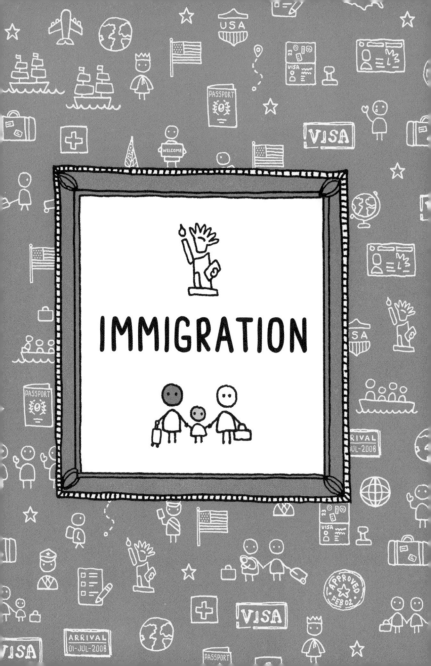

A NATION
OF IMMIGRANTS

IT IS A PROUD PRIVILEGE TO BE A CITIZEN OF THE
GREAT REPUBLIC, TO HEAR ITS SONGS SUNG, TO
REALIZE THAT WE ARE THE DESCENDANTS OF 40
MILLION PEOPLE WHO LEFT OTHER COUNTRIES, OTHER
FAMILIAR SCENES, TO COME HERE TO THE UNITED
STATES TO BUILD A NEW LIFE, TO MAKE A NEW
OPPORTUNITY FOR THEMSELVES AND THEIR CHILDREN.

I THINK IT IS NOT A BURDEN, BUT A PRIVILEGE TO
HAVE THE CHANCE IN 1963 TO SHARE THAT GREAT
CONCEPT WHICH THEY FELT SO DEEPLY AMONG ALL
OF OUR PEOPLE, TO MAKE THIS REALLY, AS IT
WAS FOR THEM, A NEW WORLD, A NEW WORLD FOR
US, AND, INDEED, FOR ALL THOSE WHO LOOK TO US.

THAT IS WHAT THIS ORGANIZATION HAS STOOD FOR
FOR 50 YEARS. THAT IS WHAT THIS COUNTRY
HAS STOOD FOR FOR 200 YEARS, AND THAT IS
WHAT THIS COUNTRY WILL CONTINUE TO STAND FOR.

PRESIDENT JOHN F. KENNEDY
50TH ANNUAL MEETING OF THE ANTI-DEFAMATION LEAGUE
JANUARY 31, 1963

WHEN	30,000 TO 10,000 YEARS AGO	1500

WHO
PEOPLE FROM EUROASIA

WHY
EXPLORATION

HOW
THERE WAS A LAND
BRIDGE BETWEEN
SIBERIA AND ALASKA

WHERE
- NORTH AMERICA
- CENTRAL AMERICA
- SOUTH AMERICA

COLONIZATION

IS THE ESTABLISHMENT OF A COLONY IN ONE
TERRITORY BY A POLITICAL POWER FROM
ANOTHER TERRITORY, AND THE SUBSEQUENT
MAINTENANCE, EXPANSION, AND EXPLOITATION
OF THAT COLONY. IT INVOLVES UNEQUAL
RELATIONSHIPS BETWEEN THE COLONIAL POWER
AND THE COLONY AND OFTEN BETWEEN THE
COLONISTS AND THE INDIGENOUS PEOPLES.

WHO
SPANISH, PORTUGUESE,
FRENCH, ITALIAN,
AND ENGLISH

WHY
COLONIZATION

WHERE
WHAT IS NOW KNOWN AS:
- ALABAMA
- LOUISIANA
- MISSISSIPPI
- FLORIDA
- CALIFORNIA
- TEXAS
- NEW MEXICO
- ARIZONA
- NEW YORK

1607

WHO
ENGLISH

WHY
COLONIZATION

WHERE
WHAT IS NOW KNOWN
AS JAMESTOWN,
VIRGINIA, AND
LATER MARYLAND

1620

WHO
ENGLISH PILGRIMS

WHY
RELIGIOUS FREEDOM

WHERE
WHAT IS NOW
KNOWN AS:
· MASSACHUSETTS
· CONNECTICUT
· RHODE ISLAND
· NEW HAMPSHIRE

1626

WHO
DUTCH

WHY
UNITED EAST
INDIAN COMPANY
COMMERCE

WHERE
WHAT IS NOW
KNOWN AS:
· NEW YORK CITY
· ALBANY

I TOLD YOU!
I KNEW HOW TO
GET TO ASIA!!!

1630

WHO
ENGLISH
PURITANS

WHY
RELIGIOUS
FREEDOM

WHERE
WHAT IS NOW
KNOWN AS
MASSACHUSETTS

1638

WHO
SWEDES AND FINNS

WHY
COLONIZATION
AND TRADE

WHERE
THE COLONY OF
NEW SWEDEN
WAS A GROUP OF
SMALL FARMS
AND SETTLEMENTS
ESTABLISHED IN
WHAT IS NOW KNOWN
AS DELAWARE,
NEW JERSEY,
PENNSYLVANIA,
AND MARYLAND

1681

WHO
ENGLISH QUAKERS

WHY
TO SPREAD THEIR
BELIEFS AND ESCAPE
PERSECUTION

WHERE
WHAT IS NOW
KNOWN AS:
• PENNSYLVANIA
• RHODE ISLAND
• NEW JERSEY

1708

1710

WHO
GERMAN PALATINES

WHY
ECONOMIC
OPPORTUNITY

WHERE
WHAT IS NOW
KNOWN AS:
• NEW YORK
• NEW JERSEY
• NORTH CAROLINA

WHO
SCOTCH-IRISH
(ULSTER-SCOTS)

WHY
RELIGIOUS FREEDOM AND
ECONOMIC OPPORTUNITY

WHERE
WHAT IS NOW KNOWN AS:
• PENNSYLVANIA
• VIRGINIA
• NORTH CAROLINA
• SOUTH CAROLINA
• INDIANA
• OHIO
• GEORGIA

1775   1790

UNITED STATES CENSUS OF 1790
WAS THE FIRST CENSUS OF
THE WHOLE UNITED STATES.

TOTAL POPULATION:
3,929,214 →
**NATIVE AMERICANS
WERE NOT IDENTIFIED
IN THE CENSUS**

PEOPLE BORN IN OTHER COUNTRIES LIVING IN THE UNITED STATES BY 1790

AFRICAN: 360,000
ENGLISH: 230,000
SCOTCH-IRISH: 135,000
GERMAN: 103,000
SCOTTISH: 48,500
IRISH: 8,000
DUTCH: 6,000
WELSH: 4,000
FRENCH: 3,000
SWEDISH: 500
OTHER: 50,000

THE NATURALIZATION ACT OF 1790
TO APPLY FOR CITIZENSHIP
YOU MUST BE A FREE WHITE
PERSON OF GOOD MORAL
CHARACTER WHO HAS LIVED
IN THE UNITED STATES FOR A
MINIMUM OF TWO YEARS.

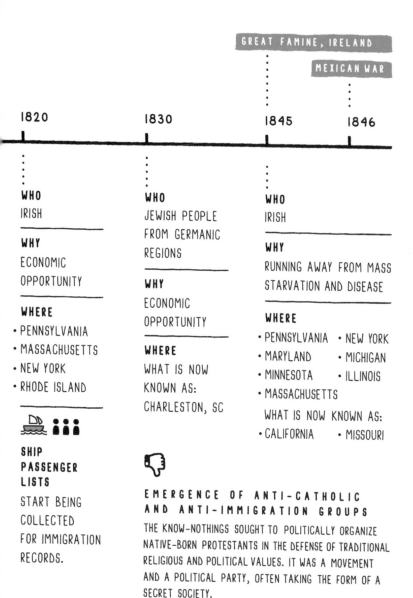

GREAT FAMINE, IRELAND

MEXICAN WAR

| 1820 | 1830 | 1845 | 1846 |

WHO
IRISH

WHY
ECONOMIC OPPORTUNITY

WHERE
- PENNSYLVANIA
- MASSACHUSETTS
- NEW YORK
- RHODE ISLAND

SHIP PASSENGER LISTS
START BEING COLLECTED FOR IMMIGRATION RECORDS.

WHO
JEWISH PEOPLE FROM GERMANIC REGIONS

WHY
ECONOMIC OPPORTUNITY

WHERE
WHAT IS NOW KNOWN AS: CHARLESTON, SC

WHO
IRISH

WHY
RUNNING AWAY FROM MASS STARVATION AND DISEASE

WHERE
- PENNSYLVANIA   - NEW YORK
- MARYLAND   - MICHIGAN
- MINNESOTA   - ILLINOIS
- MASSACHUSETTS

WHAT IS NOW KNOWN AS:
- CALIFORNIA   - MISSOURI

EMERGENCE OF ANTI-CATHOLIC AND ANTI-IMMIGRATION GROUPS
THE KNOW-NOTHINGS SOUGHT TO POLITICALLY ORGANIZE NATIVE-BORN PROTESTANTS IN THE DEFENSE OF TRADITIONAL RELIGIOUS AND POLITICAL VALUES. IT WAS A MOVEMENT AND A POLITICAL PARTY, OFTEN TAKING THE FORM OF A SECRET SOCIETY.

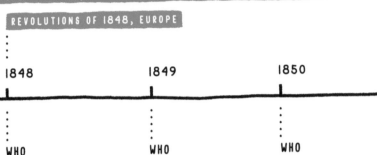

1848

1849

1850

WHO
MEXICANS

WHY
PEACE TREATY SIGNED
BY UNITED STATES
AND MEXICO

WHERE
WHAT IS NOW
KNOWN AS:
• NEW MEXICO
• CALIFORNIA

**TREATY OF
GUADALUPE HIDALGO**
GAVE AMERICAN
CITIZENSHIP TO
MEXICAN RESIDENTS
OF NEW MEXICO
AND CALIFORNIA.

WHO
EUROPEAN
ACTIVISTS AND
INTELLECTUALS
KNOWN AS THE
FORTY-EIGHTERS

WHY
EMIGRATED AFTER
THE REVOLUTIONS
OF 1848 FAILED

WHERE
• TEXAS
• OHIO
• WISCONSIN

WHO
• CHINESE
• LATIN AMERICANS
• AUSTRALIANS
• EUROPEANS

WHY
• THE GOLD RUSH
• FACTORY WORK
• RAILROADS

WHERE
• CALIFORNIA

**THE 1850
CENSUS**
WAS THE FIRST
CENSUS TO RECORD
PLACE OF BIRTH OF
THOSE BORN IN THE
UNITED STATES.

CIVIL WAR

FAMINE, SWEDEN

1861   1866   1868   1870

THE 14TH AMENDMENT

CHILDREN BORN IN THE UNITED STATES BECOME CITIZENS REGARDLESS OF THE CITIZENSHIP OF THEIR PARENTS.

WHO
SWEDES AND FINNS

WHY
FAMINE, POVERTY, AND CROP FAILURES

WHERE
- MINNESOTA
- WISCONSIN
- MICHIGAN
- OREGON
WHAT IS NOW KNOWN AS:
- WASHINGTON

 ## ANTI-CHINESE SENTIMENT

CHINESE MIGRANT WORKERS ENCOUNTERED CONSIDERABLE PREJUDICE—ESPECIALLY AT THE HANDS OF POOR WHITE PEOPLE. POLITICIANS AND LABOR LEADERS USED THEM AS SCAPEGOATS FOR THE WHITE LOWER CLASS. GROUPS AGAINST CHINESE WORKERS STARTED ORGANIZING IN CALIFORNIA.

THE NATURALIZATION ACT OF 1870

EXTENDED NATURALIZATION LAWS TO ALIENS OF AFRICAN NATIVITY AND PERSONS OF AFRICAN DESCENT.

1880

WHO
GERMANS, ENGLISH, IRISH, FRENCH-CANADIANS, ITALIANS, GREEKS, HUNGARIANS, AND POLES

WHY
- STEAM-POWERED SHIPS REPLACED SAIL SHIPS, ALLOWING FOR LOWER FARES.
- YOUNGER PEOPLE (15-30 YEARS OLD) STARTED MIGRATING TO AMERICA LOOKING FOR NEW OPPORTUNITIES.

WHERE
- NEW YORK
- PENNSYLVANIA
- ILLINOIS
- MASSACHUSETTS

1882

CHINESE EXCLUSION ACT
FEDERAL LAW PROHIBITING THE IMMIGRATION OF CHINESE LABORERS INTO THE UNITED STATES.

1892

ELLIS ISLAND 1892-1954
MORE THAN 12 MILLION PEOPLE PASSED THROUGH THIS IMMIGRATION INSPECTION STATION DURING ITS YEARS OF OPERATION.

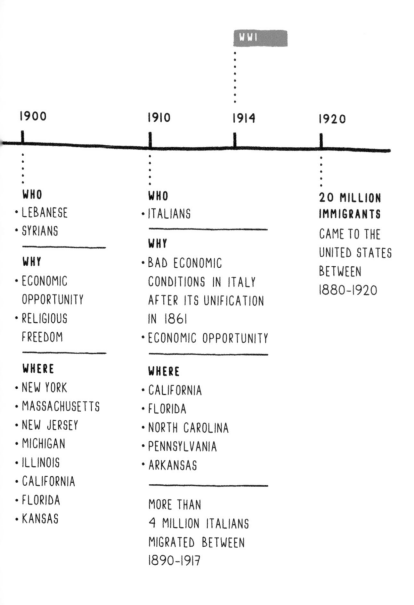

WWI

1900　　　1910　　1914　　　1920

WHO
- LEBANESE
- SYRIANS

WHY
- ECONOMIC
  OPPORTUNITY
- RELIGIOUS
  FREEDOM

WHERE
- NEW YORK
- MASSACHUSETTS
- NEW JERSEY
- MICHIGAN
- ILLINOIS
- CALIFORNIA
- FLORIDA
- KANSAS

WHO
- ITALIANS

WHY
- BAD ECONOMIC
  CONDITIONS IN ITALY
  AFTER ITS UNIFICATION
  IN 1861
- ECONOMIC OPPORTUNITY

WHERE
- CALIFORNIA
- FLORIDA
- NORTH CAROLINA
- PENNSYLVANIA
- ARKANSAS

MORE THAN
4 MILLION ITALIANS
MIGRATED BETWEEN
1890-1917

**20 MILLION
IMMIGRANTS**
CAME TO THE
UNITED STATES
BETWEEN
1880-1920

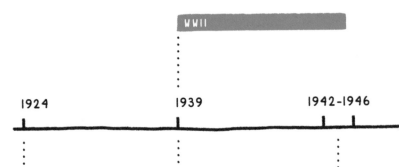

WWII

| 1924 | 1939 | 1942–1946 |

IMMIGRATION ACT OF 1924
(THE JOHNSON-REED ACT)

- LIMITED THE NUMBER OF IMMIGRANTS USING A NATIONAL ORIGIN QUOTA.
- IT BENEFITED NORTHERN AND WESTERN EUROPEANS AND DISCRIMINATED AGAINST IMMIGRANTS FROM ASIA, SOUTHERN EUROPE, AND LATIN AMERICA.

- FEWER PASSENGER LINES CROSSED THE ATLANTIC OCEAN DURING THE WAR.
- INTRODUCTION OF STRICTER VISA PROCESSES TO COME INTO THE UNITED STATES.

JAPANESE INTERNMENT IN AMERICA

- THE FORCED RELOCATION OF APPROXIMATELY 120,000 PEOPLE OF JAPANESE ANCESTRY, 62 PERCENT OF WHOM WERE AMERICAN CITIZENS, TO LABOR CAMPS.
- THE ACTIONS WERE AUTHORIZED BY PRESIDENT FRANKLIN D. ROOSEVELT TWO MONTHS AFTER JAPAN'S ATTACK ON PEARL HARBOR.

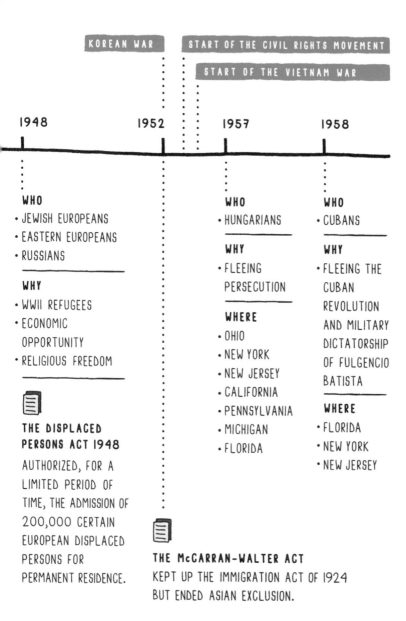

KOREAN WAR

START OF THE CIVIL RIGHTS MOVEMENT

START OF THE VIETNAM WAR

| 1948 | 1952 | 1957 | 1958 |

WHO
- JEWISH EUROPEANS
- EASTERN EUROPEANS
- RUSSIANS

WHY
- WWII REFUGEES
- ECONOMIC OPPORTUNITY
- RELIGIOUS FREEDOM

THE DISPLACED PERSONS ACT 1948

AUTHORIZED, FOR A LIMITED PERIOD OF TIME, THE ADMISSION OF 200,000 CERTAIN EUROPEAN DISPLACED PERSONS FOR PERMANENT RESIDENCE.

THE McCARRAN-WALTER ACT
KEPT UP THE IMMIGRATION ACT OF 1924 BUT ENDED ASIAN EXCLUSION.

WHO
- HUNGARIANS

WHY
- FLEEING PERSECUTION

WHERE
- OHIO
- NEW YORK
- NEW JERSEY
- CALIFORNIA
- PENNSYLVANIA
- MICHIGAN
- FLORIDA

WHO
- CUBANS

WHY
- FLEEING THE CUBAN REVOLUTION AND MILITARY DICTATORSHIP OF FULGENCIO BATISTA

WHERE
- FLORIDA
- NEW YORK
- NEW JERSEY

VIETNAM WAR

CIVIL RIGHTS MOVEMENT

1965

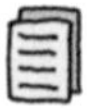

THE IMMIGRATION AND NATIONALITY ACT (HART-CELLER ACT)

- PRODUCT OF THE CIVIL RIGHTS.
- ABOLISHED THE QUOTA SYSTEM BASED ON NATIONAL ORIGINS.
- IT FOCUSED ON FAMILY RELATIONSHIPS WITH U.S. CITIZENS AND IMMIGRANT SKILLS.

1978

WHO

- VIETNAMESE
- CAMBODIAN

WHY

- ECONOMIC OPPORTUNITY
- WAR REFUGEES

WHERE

- CALIFORNIA
- TEXAS
- OHIO
- MASSACHUSETTS
- RHODE ISLAND
- WASHINGTON
- OREGON

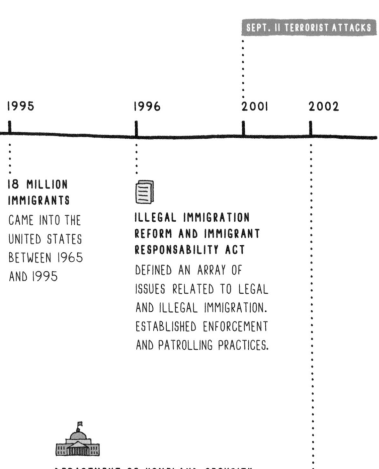

SEPT. II TERRORIST ATTACKS

1995   1996   2001   2002

**18 MILLION
IMMIGRANTS**
CAME INTO THE
UNITED STATES
BETWEEN 1965
AND 1995

**ILLEGAL IMMIGRATION
REFORM AND IMMIGRANT
RESPONSABILITY ACT**
DEFINED AN ARRAY OF
ISSUES RELATED TO LEGAL
AND ILLEGAL IMMIGRATION.
ESTABLISHED ENFORCEMENT
AND PATROLLING PRACTICES.

DEPARTMENT OF HOMELAND SECURITY
CREATED IN RESPONSE TO THE SEPTEMBER II TERRORIST ATTACKS.
RESPONSIBLE FOR PUBLIC SECURITY, ANTI-TERRORISM, BORDER
SECURITY, IMMIGRATION, CUSTOMS, CYBERSECURITY, AND DISASTER
PREVENTION AND MANAGEMENT.

TOTAL POPULATION
OF THE UNITED STATES

323.1 MILLION

**WHAT LANGUAGE IS
SPOKEN AT HOME?** . . . .

85.3
MILLION

SPEAK OTHER LANGUAGES:

40.5 MILLION SPANISH

3.4 MILLION CHINESE

1.7 MILLION TAGALOG

1.5 MILLION VIETNAMESE

1.2 MILLION ARABIC

1.2 MILLION FRENCH

1.1 MILLION KOREAN

0.91 MILLION RUSSIAN

0.91 MILLION GERMAN

0.86 MILLION HAITIAN CREOLE

32 MILLION OTHER

237.8
MILLION
SPEAK ENGLISH

43.3 MILLION
IMMIGRANTS

20.7 MILLION
NATURALIZED
U.S. CITIZENS

22.6 MILLION

- PERMANENT RESIDENTS
  (GREEN CARD HOLDERS)
- RESIDENTS WITH
  TEMPORARY VISAS
  (STUDENTS AND WORKERS)
- UNAUTHORIZED IMMIGRANTS

VISAS

HAVING A U.S. VISA ALLOWS A FOREIGNER TO TRAVEL TO A PORT OF ENTRY, AIRPORT, OR LAND BORDER CROSSING AND REQUEST PERMISSION TO ENTER THE UNITED STATES.

HAVING A VISA DOES NOT GUARANTEE ENTRY. A U.S. CUSTOMS AND BORDER SECURITY OFFICIAL CAN DENY ADMISSION.

VISAS ARE PRINTED INSIDE YOUR PASSPORT

TEMPORARY
NONIMMIGRANT

SOME OF THE PURPOSES:
- TOURISM
- INTERNATIONAL ORGANIZATIONS
- TEMPORARY WORKERS
- STUDENTS
- GOVERNMENT
- MILITARY

PERMANENT
IMMIGRANT

SOME OF THE PURPOSES:
- SPOUSES / FIANCÉ(E)S OF U.S. CITIZENS
- CHILD ADOPTION
- CERTAIN FAMILY MEMBERS OF U.S. CITIZENS AND PERMANENT RESIDENTS
- EMPLOYER SPONSORSHIP

PERMANENT RESIDENCY

TO BECOME A PERMANENT RESIDENT YOU MUST BE SPONSORED BY A FAMILY MEMBER, BE SPONSORED BY AN EMPOLYER, OBTAIN REFUGEE OR ASYLEE STATUS, OBTAIN A GREEN CARD THROUGH A LOTTERY, OR APPLY AS AN INVESTOR.

GREEN CARD

RIGHTS OF A PERMANENT RESIDENT

- LIVE AND WORK ANYWHERE IN THE U.S.
- APPLY FOR CITIZENSHIP WHEN ELIGIBLE
- REQUEST A U.S. VISA FOR YOUR PARTNER AND UNMARRIED CHILDREN
- GET SOCIAL SECURITY, SUPPLEMENTAL SECURITY INCOME, AND MEDICARE BENEFITS IF ELIGIBLE
- OWN PROPERTY IN THE U.S.
- APPLY FOR A DRIVER'S LICENSE
- LEAVE AND RETURN TO THE UNITED STATES UNDER CERTAIN CONDITIONS
- ATTEND PUBLIC SCHOOL AND COLLEGE
- JOIN CERTAIN BRANCHES OF THE UNITED STATES ARMED FORCES
- PURCHASE OR OWN A FIREARM, UNLESS THERE ARE LOCAL RESTRICTIONS

RESPONSABILITIES OF A PERMANENT RESIDENT

- OBEY ALL FEDERAL, STATE, AND LOCAL LAWS
- PAY FEDERAL, STATE, AND LOCAL TAXES
- CARRY YOUR GREEN CARD AT ALL TIMES
- REGISTER WITH THE SELECTIVE SERVICE IF YOU ARE A MALE BETWEEN 18 26 YEARS OLD
- MAINTAIN YOUR IMMIGRATION STATUS
- GIVE YOUR NEW ADDRESS TO THE DEPARTMENT OF HOMELAND SECURITY WHEN YOU MOVE

CITIZENSHIP PROCESS

1

FIND OUT IF YOU ARE ELIGIBLE.
USE THE NATURALIZATION ELIGIBILITY WORKSHEET PROVIDED BY THE GOVERNMENT

2

FILL OUT FORM **N-400**

3 SUBMIT:

 FORM N-400

+

OTHER DOCUMENTS REQUESTED

+

CHECK OR MONEY ORDER

4

ONCE YOU RECEIVE YOUR APPOINTMENT NOTICE GO TO THE **BIOMETRICS APPOINTMENT**

SIGNATURE

5 PREPARE FOR THE INTERVIEW AND
STUDY FOR THE TEST

DURING YOUR NATURALIZATION INTERVIEW, YOU WILL BE ASKED QUESTIONS ABOUT YOUR APPLICATION AND BACKGROUND. YOU WILL ALSO TAKE AN ENGLISH AND CIVICS TEST. THE ENGLISH TEST COVERS READING, WRITING, AND SPEAKING. THE CIVICS TEST COVERS THE QUESTIONS YOU MUST STUDY TO PREPARE. YOU CAN FIND THE QUESTIONS AT WWW.USCIS.GOV. MOST OF THE ANSWERS TO THESE QUESTIONS ARE COVERED IN THIS BOOK.

6 RECEIVE A DECISION FROM THE GOVERNMENT → GRANTED

DENIED

YOU ARE NOT ELIGIBLE FOR NATURALIZATION

CONTINUED

YOU NEED TO PROVIDE ADDITIONAL INFORMATION

7 TAKE THE OATH OF ALLEGIANCE TO THE UNITED STATES

8 BE AN AWESOME CITIZEN

50 STARS
ONE FOR EACH STATE

I PLEDGE ALLEGIANCE TO THE FLAG OF THE UNITED STATES OF AMERICA, AND TO THE REPUBLIC FOR WHICH IT STANDS, ONE NATION UNDER GOD, INDIVISIBLE, WITH LIBERTY AND JUSTICE FOR ALL.

13 STRIPES
TO REPRESENT THE ORIGINAL COLONIES

PLEDGE OF ALLEGIANCE
IT'S AN EXPRESSION OF LOYALTY TO THE FLAG AND TO THE UNITED STATES OF AMERICA.

FIRST STANZA

O SAY CAN YOU SEE, BY THE DAWN'S EARLY LIGHT,
WHAT SO PROUDLY WE HAIL'D AT THE TWILIGHT'S LAST GLEAMING?
WHOSE BROAD STRIPES AND BRIGHT STARS THROUGH THE PERILOUS FIGHT
O'ER THE RAMPARTS WE WATCH'D, WERE SO GALLANTLY STREAMING?
AND THE ROCKET'S RED GLARE, THE BOMBS BURSTING IN AIR,
GAVE PROOF THROUGH THE NIGHT THAT OUR FLAG WAS STILL THERE,
O SAY DOES THAT STAR-SPANGLED BANNER YET WAVE
O'ER THE LAND OF THE FREE AND THE HOME OF THE BRAVE?

4TH ★
OF
JULY

INDEPENDENCE DAY

WHEN YOU
BECOME A CITIZEN

YOU PROMISE TO:

BE LOYAL TO THE UNITED STATES,
OBEY AND DEFEND THE CONSTITUTION
AND LAWS OF THE UNITED STATES,
GIVE UP LOYALTY TO OTHER COUNTRIES,
SERVE THE NATION,
AND SERVE IN THE MILITARY
WHEN REQUIRED BY THE LAW.

DEDICATION

To my parents, Mami, Boby, and Loly
and to my grandmas, Viqui and Mama.

ACKNOWLEDGMENTS

Thank you, Chung Liang, for introducing me to great people. Thank you, Tom Lichtenheld, for all of your generous help and advice. Thank you, Amy Rennert, for believing in my project and for your expertise. I am very lucky to have crossed paths with you.

I want to thank my editor, Samantha Weiner, and all the people at Abrams that made this book happen. I have a beautiful book because of you all.

Thank you, Kim Sullivan and Clayton Brown, for all the edits, revisions, additions, and conversations. You are the best American friends an immigrant could have. Thank you for making my book better.

Other great friends that were happy to help: Toshihiro Fujimura, Liz Kores, John Mallett, and Jennifer Ross. Thank you!

Thank you, Gioco Roesch and Jodi Vrable Faulkner, for being on the other side of the phone when, so many times, I needed to laugh or cry during this process.

EDITOR: SAMANTHA WEINER
DESIGN MANAGER: DEVIN GROSZ
DESIGNER: SILVIA HIDALGO
PRODUCTION MANAGER: MICHAEL KASERKIE

LIBRARY OF CONGRESS CONTROL NUMBER: 2017956793

ISBN: 978-1-4197-3075-7
eISBN: 978-1-68335-341-6
JUNIOR LIBRARY GUILD EDITION: 978-1-4197-3660-5

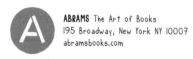

ABRAMS The Art of Books
195 Broadway, New York NY 10007
abramsbooks.com